Do you Believe?

Do you Believe?

Contemporary Insight on the Question of Faith

WILLIAM BROWNSON

ZONDERVAN
PUBLISHING HOUSE
OF THE ZONDERVAN CORPORATION | GRAND RAPIDS MICHIGAN 49506

To
MY DAD
a loving father,
a good man,
and
a fellow-believer

CONTENTS

FOREWORD

Is the question of *believing* a live, and perhaps perplexing one for you? "What can a person believe today about God, about Jesus Christ? And how can I come to a meaningful personal faith?"

If those questions are in any sense yours, then the Gospel according to John is a book addressed to your situation. And these thoughts from that book are especially meant for you.

"Would you believe . . . ?" Read awhile, and think awhile. Then face the big question head-on, "*Do* you believe . . . ?" It could mean a fresh beginning. More than that, it could start a new life.

"These things are written that you might believe . . . and that believing, you might have life . . . ."

Do you Believe?

1. Christmas: Is It Just for the Kids?

The true light that enlightens every man was coming into the world. He was in the world, and the world was made through him, yet the world knew him not. He came to his own home, and his own people received him not. But to all who received him, who believed in his name, he gave power to become children of God; who were born, not of blood nor of the will of the flesh nor of the will of man, but of God.

(John 1:9-13)

"CHRISTMAS IS FOR the kids," quipped an acquaintance of mine recently. He was observing that it always seems to be the children who enjoy Christmas most. Since his little flock had long since grown up and left the family fold, he found that Christmas "just wasn't the same any more." Many of us perhaps will know what he meant. What a treat it is to be around the small ones at Christmas time; to catch the thrill of their expectancy; to see their wide-eyed surprise and delight; to watch chubby pink fingers tugging away at ribbons and wrappings! That has to be one of the special joys of Christmas. But soon, too soon, the children are gone and something else has gone with them. With a trace of wistfulness we find ourselves saying, "Christmas is for the kids."

9

Maybe someone looks back today at childhood holidays long past and recalls how much more Christmas meant then than it does now. Now there are few surprises to anticipate; little of the tingling thrill remains; and the sheer busyness of getting ready for Christmas seems more of a burden than a joy. Christmas is for the kids.

When others say it, it has a sadder meaning. For them, childhood's faith has long fled and with it its fresh innocence. They are sophisticated now. The Christmas story that seemed so real then seems too old, too bland, too familiar to kindle much enthusiasm or make much difference any more. To "a world come of age," as they say, Christmas is for the kids.

Well, is that all there is to say? Is that the hard fact we have to face, that the gladness of Christmas wanes with the years? Hardly. At least not for everyone. There are some for whom its meaning grows richer and its joys, though less exuberant, more deep and full. There are many of you who are ready to say, "Yes, Christmas is for the kids; but not just for them. It's for us, for all of us." Why then do some seem to lose the joy — or never find it at all? How does Christmas become trivial and wonderless for us? Perhaps there are many reasons. Let me suggest three.

First, we may fail to grasp what really happened at Christmas. Do you know what that was? The Apostle John, one of the men who knew Jesus best, writes in the opening words of his gospel that "the true light that enlightens every man was coming into the world." For him, something happened on that first Christmas that was altogether astonishing. The true Light, the true Life, the true God was coming into the world. John is saying that the God who made the galaxies came down to this planet and became a baby. The truth behind every truth, the life that quickens all life, was somehow bundled in a manger bed. The everlasting Word that spoke everything into being became the flesh and blood of a tiny boy. That was Christmas. And the whole Christian story stands or falls with it.

There are some, of course, who understand this claim and reject it out of hand. "Preposterous!" they say. "Ridiculous! The thing is impossible." However we may feel about that reaction, we can surely understand it. What could be stranger to believe than that God Almighty should become the son of a peasant girl? Nothing ever dreamed up in science fiction could be as mind-boggling as that. No wonder some people thought that Jesus was crazy when He made the claim to be one with the Father.

But what can be said about people to whom the news of Christmas seems tame and tepid? I have to believe that they don't know what it means. As Dorothy Sayers, the English playwright-theologian, put it, "We may call that doctrine exhilarating or we may call it devastating; we may call it revelation or we may call it rubbish; but if we call it dull then words have no meaning at all." Just let your mind roam across this terrain for a minute. For whatever reason God chose to make human beings, to expose them to sorrow and temptations, to sufferings and death, whatever He had in mind by that, He showed Himself willing to share their lot. He came to be with us and more — to be one of us. To believe that is to enter a new world of worship and wonder. Whatever else Christmas may be for us then, it can never be trivial or commonplace.

I see another reason why Christmas loses its dimension of depth for people. We have sometimes ignored its note of tragedy. The popularizers of Christmas have often caricatured it — made it seem unreal. The circumstances of Jesus' birth have been hopelessly sentimentalized. Babies just aren't born with halos and stables don't glow with soft light. But there is a type of religion that admires Jesus as a beautiful infant, a holy child, and in fancy keeps Him so. Who would not love this baby of Bethlehem and rejoice at His coming?

11

For the Apostle John, however, the joy of that birthday was already tinged with pathos. The inn had no room for Him then, as the world had none later. "He was in the world," writes John, "and the world was made through him, yet the world knew him not." It did not recognize Him, did not acknowledge His coming. It was as though a great king had found no welcome in his own realm. God came to His "home," the world which He had fashioned, and to His own people, those whom He had especially chosen; and they refused to receive Him.

Isn't that the most poignant kind of heartbreak for any of us? We can take it when strangers reject us. After all, they don't know us — what more could we expect from them? But when you come back to your own hometown and are greeted with silence, when familiar faces look quickly away, and when even old friends no longer open their homes and hearts to you, that is a special kind of agony. Christmas began it for Jesus. The miracle of God's coming was met with an almost greater marvel — His rejection at our hands. The angels sang of "peace on earth" and "men of good will," but Jesus encountered something quite different. The earth plotted war against Him and men set their wills to do Him in. Our leading authorities in church and state considered Him a man too dangerous to have around. We bribed one of His friends to arrange for His arrest. We tried Him on trumped-up charges. We had Him publicly beaten and hanged as a criminal. All that was ahead for Him on that first Christmas.

We can treat it matter-of-factly or with shallow merriment only when this bittersweet message has not probed the conscience, only when we separate Jesus the child from Christ the rejected One, the crucified. When the light of Christmas seems dim to us, we may have forgotten how dark our world is without it. Forgetting how the world treated Him and how much we are a part of that world, we sometimes vainly dream that we did not need His coming very badly. So Christmas comes and goes and we never know "the soul's despair or its breathless gratitude."

Here is a third reason for apathy toward the wonder of Christmas. Not only do we fail to grasp what happened when God came to us, not only do we forget how dismally we treated Him; we've missed the mark in gratitude, too. Most of us have scarcely begun to appreciate the gift He came to bring. He gave to men, John tells us, "power to become children of God." Have you thought about what that gift means?

What kind of gift means most to you? There are some, of course, that don't really seem like gifts. The "useful" kind, for example. Johnny wants a basketball but his parents buy him a new coat instead because that's *useful*. Johnny is no fool. He knows that Mom and Dad wanted him to have that coat and that they would have bought it for him sooner or later anyway. Somehow it doesn't seem to him like a gift. Or suppose someone gives you a gift with definite instructions about how it is to be used, with strings attached. Or suppose they don't seem very happy about giving it. Under those conditions, gifts don't bring us much joy.

What all of that says to me is that gifts, though we all want them, don't in themselves satisfy us. We're listening for a message with the gift. We're looking for a giver behind it. We want desperately to know that we're cared about, esteemed, loved. That's why we like gifts that surprise us — they show that we are special to the giver. He has been thinking about us and knows we are unique. We like gifts also that are freely given, the ones that people weren't obligated or pressured to give. They mean that someone found real pleasure just in giving to us. Most of all, we like a gift in which a person shares with us something of himself. I read once about a busy executive who put a note in his little girl's Christmas stocking, promising her an hour of his time each day. There's a gift to be treasured!

If there ever was a giver who gave like that, it's the

Lord who came at Christmas. He gave us "power to become children of God." What a surprise! A new birth, a new beginning, a new life for people who have bungled badly. He knew we needed that! How often we've wished that somehow we could start again! And more than that — a new *relationship:* life as God's child, in His family, at home with Him. How good that sounds! We've been wanderers and orphans too long.

And talk about a gift that is free, undeserved, unexpected! Why, this Jesus loves the very world that had no room for Him. He seeks those who spurned Him. He dies for the sake of those who caused His death and, once risen from the dead, He offers to *them* His great gift. What generosity! We could never earn that new birth, pay for it, achieve it, or bring it about in any human way. It's His totally new creation, given to those who have no reason or right to expect it.

But more still. This gift supremely brings with it the Giver. To receive it means to receive Him, the living Lord. He comes personally to us, shares with us His sonship to the Father, imparts to us His own risen life. Believe it — when He came to us at Christmas, He held nothing back. He gave Himself.

I ask you, would it be possible to pass off Christmas with a shrug or a yawn if you really believed that? Maybe that's the problem. Perhaps we've never known what it is to receive the gift, to believe in His name. No wonder Christmas doesn't mean more — or means less now than it did before. But this Christmas can be different. If today you welcome Jesus Christ as the Lord who came for you, who suffered for you, and who lives now to give you life, then you will really know Christmas. You may even say with a new wealth of meaning, "Christmas is for the kids." But now you're past nostalgia. Now it has nothing to do with years or inches. Christmas with all its depth of joy and wonder is for those who trust in Jesus — for God's grateful children.

1. How have your feelings about Christmas changed with the passing of the years?

2. What, according to John, is the central meaning of the Christmas event? How do you think people will be affected who clearly grasp this meaning?

3. How do you account for the opposition and rejection which Jesus received when He came among us?

4. According to John, how do people become "children of God"? What meanings does this phrase suggest to you?

2. What's New in Religion?

And the Word became flesh and dwelt among us, full of grace and truth; we have beheld his glory, glory as of the only Son from the Father. (John bore witness to him, and cried, "This was he of whom I said, 'He who comes after me ranks before me, for he was before me.'") And from his fulness have we all received, grace upon grace. For the law was given through Moses; grace and truth came through Jesus Christ. No one has ever seen God; the only Son, who is in the bosom of the Father, he has made him known.

(John 1:14-18)

WHAT'S NEW? THAT question always generates a special kind of interest. The "new" seems to attract us. In fact, we call anything we find particularly striking — news. Why this fascination with newness, this absorbing interest in the latest thing? Is the new more important than the old?

The advertisers seem determined to make us think so. How they belabor that word *new!* Everything, apparently, has to be new if it's expected to sell. If the word itself does not appear in the name of the product — "New Whatsit" — we are at least told that this is a new model or a new formula or has been transformed by an

16

amazing new additive. Usually the new ingredient has made it so remarkable and revolutionary that no one in his right mind would ever want the old again!

Now all of us take that kind of advertising with more than a grain of salt. We know it can't be all that new, but still we perk up our ears. It isn't simply that we want to keep up with the Joneses, though that ambition is strongly encouraged. It is partly our trust in the amazing technology of our society. We have seen again and again how modern skills, by refining the old, can make it better. Every now and then, when something breaks down, we grumble that things aren't made like they used to be; but few of us act consistently on that belief. We may treasure antiques for esthetic reasons, but if we want to go somewhere or do something or meet some practical need, most of us want the newest aids available.

But what is true for goods and gadgets, for machines and medicines, may not be true across the board. The newest is not always the best. Think of the arts, for example. What someone splashed on a canvas yesterday will probably not make the world forget Michelangelo or da Vinci. And although the man who wrote *The Greening of America* feels that Beethoven's Ninth Symphony can't match the Rolling Stones, not everyone is ready to agree with him. History certainly teaches us that new governments, born in revolution, are not always better or less tyrannical than those they replace. When it comes to persons, or to the realm of ideas and human values, newness does not guarantee superiority. It may not even represent progress.

We need especially to remember that, I think, when we deal with religious life and belief. Ours seems to be a time of religious novelty. The question "What's new in religion?" is certainly a live one on the contemporary scene. There is much that claims to be new and implicitly, at least, to be better. New theologies have become about as regular in appearance as car models.

Perhaps more widely discussed than any of them is the phenomenon called "the New Morality." These viewpoints are often set forth with the unexamined assumption that the new is bound to be better, truer, more worthwhile than the old.

Some interpret that kind of attitude in the light of the generation gap. Many of our youth are fed up with the traditions, the ideals, the life styles of the older generation. Anything that sounds different, so the argument runs, they are ready to embrace. They are conditioned from the start to be suspicious of the old and enthusiastic about the new. But true as that may be in some cases, it can't be the whole story. For most, at any rate, the religious quest is more than a reaction against the establishment. There are always some who are novelty shoppers in religion, but most people who search for the new are those who simply haven't found fulfillment and meaning in the religion they have known.

The magazine *Psychology Today* recently carried a perceptive analysis of what is called the counter-culture. The author of the article sees a deep religious impulse behind it. The ethical dimension of religion may often be ignored, together with its call for a transcendent commitment, so that what results sometimes is mere "religiosity." But it all expresses, in the words of the writer, the "convulsive gasp of a culture that cries out for transcendence and meaning." Many, in response to this inner cry, are seeking a kind of chemical transcendence through drugs, or spiritual repose in some world-escaping form of religion. These, too, betray a poignant longing for something better than they have found. Mere novelty, of course, is not enough. For most of us it isn't simply something new we long for, but what will make *us* new, what can make *us* different, what can transform these lives of ours.

I guess that's what we all look for from time to time. Listen to this word from a first-century believer. "The law was given through Moses; grace and truth came

18

through Jesus Christ." He was giving his witness as to what can make us new people — and what can't.

What can't make us new people? The law, any law, even God's law. The first Christians were those who had been trained in the Old Testament Scriptures. They knew the law of Moses — over six hundred commandments' worth. A generous half of them were positive instructions; the rest, prohibitions of various kinds. They honored this law as having come from God. They knew it represented His will. Many of them made heroic efforts to obey it, but they found it had no transforming power for them. It could point out their errors, it could show them the right way, but it made nothing new. Hence it was both a blessing and a burden. The Apostle Peter could call it a "yoke upon the neck . . . which neither our fathers nor we have been able to bear" (Acts 15:10).

Haven't we all found it so with the law we have known? Everyone has a deep sense within him of what he ought to do, and all the great religions of the world have provided men with genuine insight about what the good life involves. For that we can be profoundly thankful. We never totally lose the vision of what life is meant to be. That sense of "oughtness" which never disappears is one of God's good gifts.

But what can the law, even God's law, do for us today? It can tell us something about what the past has been like — how far short we have fallen, how many opportunities to do good we've missed. It can point out our pettiness, our sham, our ingratitude, and hardness. It can make us wince by reminding us of the people we've hurt, or make us blush at the secret shame we've known. It can say, "This is how you ought to live; this is the kind of person you must be," but that is all it can do. We may try to stifle its voice or we may make a pretense of keeping it, but in neither case do we find in it a power to make us different. Who wouldn't cry out for something more, especially when life's brevity strikes home to us, when an old year is dying and a new one is about to be born?

Grace is the word for it. Grace is what we need. To have all our faults and failings forgiven and to experience a power that transforms us — that is grace. And Christians find that in Jesus Christ. "We have beheld his glory," says John, "glory as of the only Son from the Father, full of grace and truth." "And from his fulness have we all received, grace upon grace." This is the old gift that makes people new. It's the ever new reality of Christian faith.

Let me express how this grace, this gift of Christ, seems unique to me. I can think of myself in my failures to keep the law, my blunders and bunglings and downright meanness, as a man who has fallen into a pit. Try as I may, I can't get out; and the walls are caving in all around me. Suddenly a face appears above me. "I see you down there," comes a voice. "I warned you. If you had done what I told you, you never would have fallen in there." That's the voice of the law. That's all it can say. Soon another man appears with this good advice: "All right, get busy, apply yourself, and you'll soon be out of there." That's the law speaking again through the voice of do-it-yourself religion. "Just grab your own boots and pull!" While I'm vainly struggling to get out, I hear still another voice: "I know it seems like you're down in that pit, but don't believe it. It's all in your mind. There is no pit!" That's a religion that denies reality — and leaves me where I am. But then along comes a man who clambers down in the pit with me, delivers me from it, and gives me strength to live a new life.

That's the grace of Jesus Christ. His first disciples could see it in the way He forgave a condemned woman, or befriended outcasts, or healed and transformed broken people. They saw it in His self-giving love even to death — death on a cross. They experienced it personally in His kind, patient ministry to them. Grace is

20

the unmerited love that freely forgives and makes a new beginning possible. Grace is the power of the risen Christ at work in our lives, making all things new. Problems don't disappear of course and struggles don't end, but God does begin a new thing in our lives. He gives us power to become the children of God.

Yes, grace and *truth*. Truth also came by Jesus Christ. There is much truth elsewhere, but always in bits and pieces, gleams and glimpses. The truth of which John speaks is the truth of God, God's own self-revealing. "No one has ever seen God," writes John. "The only Son, who is in the bosom of the Father, he has made him known." The heart of the message is not merely that Jesus is like God, but that God is like Jesus. In the past God had said many things to the world through prophets and holy men; but now His very being, mind, and will have been embodied in Jesus — in His lowly, suffering, self-giving humanity. He is "God's self-utterance to men, God's language and living thought, God's eloquence, God's truth in action, the measure of God's mind." In His kind of humanness, God's glory stands revealed.

How can this become real for us? By looking steadily at Jesus Christ as He is made known in Scripture and in the witness of His people. Hear John's witness: "We have beheld his glory, glory as of the only Son from the Father." Look toward Him — living, loving, dying, rising again, alive forever. To gaze at Christ in faith is to realize that the God who gave the law is the God who gives His Son. It is to know His Father heart. This is the truth that makes us free — to know that in Christ God is a Father to us, forgiving and renewing. This is the ever fresh wonder of the Christian faith and our hope for a really new beginning in life. To accept the grace Christ offers and believe the truth He brings, is to begin again with joyful hope.

QUESTIONS FOR DISCUSSION

1. Why does "newness" have such a powerful appeal? What qualities do we usually associate with the word "new"?

2. In what ways can the preoccupation with "newness" mislead us?

3. What are the really new things which Christ brought to the world?

4. Where do you most see the need for newness in your life?

3. See for Yourself!

The next day Jesus decided to go to Galilee. And he found Philip and said to him, "Follow me." Now Philip was from Bethsaida, the city of Andrew and Peter. Philip found Nathanael, and said to him, "We have found him of whom Moses in the law and also the prophets wrote, Jesus of Nazareth, the son of Joseph." Nathanael said to him, "Can anything good come out of Nazareth?" Philip said to him, "Come and see."

(John 1:43-46)

WHEN YOU FIND the thing you're looking for, you can't keep it to yourself. The thrill of discovery simply has to be shared. Remember the story about Archimedes, the Greek inventor? It seems that the king of Syracuse had presented him with a tough problem. A crown had been prepared for him which was supposed to be pure gold, but the king had a troubling suspicion that some silver had been mixed with it. How could he tell? Archimedes was mulling this over one day as he stepped into the water at the public baths and noticed how it overflowed. Could this be a way of detecting whether an alloy had been added to the crown? Suppose he put the crown and then equal weights of gold and of silver separately into a vessel of water and noted the differences of overflow. That would do it! Archimedes was so overjoyed when this thought came to him that he ran home without his clothes on, shouting, "Eureka! Eureka!" (I have found it! I have found it!) Word about that discovery must have spread fast!

News of a big "find" always gets around. When gold was found in California in 1849, it wasn't long before everyone knew about it and thousands were heading west as fast as they could go. Oil strikes and uranium finds don't remain secrets for very long either.

This is true also in the more personal discoveries we make. Jesus told delightful stories about a woman searching for lost money and a shepherd out after his wandering sheep. In each case, when the search was finally successful, the happy finder called together friends and neighbors and said, "Rejoice with me, for I have found what I had lost." That kind of gladness needs to be passed along in order to be fully enjoyed. As a great preacher once put it, "A joy that tells its story is like some imprisoned bird that has found the sunny air of larger spaces."

To share our find with someone else is to multiply its meaning for us. You've experienced that many times, haven't you? When some long-deferred hope was finally realized, you couldn't wait to tell the people who meant most to you, those who you knew could enter into the joy you felt. I can recall happy experiences in my work as a pastor, when God's power touched someone's life, after which I almost raced home to tell my wife. I was scarcely in the door before I was sharing with her what had happened.

Now that is especially true of life's greatest discovery, the finding of what every human heart most deeply longs for: a meeting with God in Jesus Christ. The first finding, of course, is His. He is yearning over us before we begin to look for Him. He is the seeker of lost sheep, the Father running to meet wayward children. But we still know a moment of genuine discovery when we become aware of His love and meet Him face to face in Jesus Christ. From that moment on, we are witnesses.

That's what happened in the case of Philip, one of Jesus' first disciples. One day on His way to Galilee, Jesus found Philip and said to him, "Follow me." Once found by the Lord, the next thing Philip did was to find his friend Nathanael and tell him the good news. "We have found him of whom Moses in the law and also the prophets wrote, Jesus of Nazareth." In other words, "We have found the One God's promises are all about, the One we've been waiting for, the One in whom all our hopes will find fulfillment. We have found Him. It's Jesus."

That is simply put, but it expresses profoundly what went on in the early growth of the Christian movement and what is still going on today. One person somewhere along the road of life is found and met and called by Jesus Christ. He finds in Christ the answer for his life, the end of his quest, the satisfaction for longings he could never fully express before; and that sense of discovery sends him out to tell the persons he knows best.

I'll never forget sitting on a curbstone under a street light in a small New York village while a high school friend told me how I could know Jesus Christ in a personal way. It all sounded new and wonderful to me, although I had often attended church and Sunday school. When I got home that night it was very late, but I woke up my parents anyway. I had to tell them what I had found. And you know, the joy of that discovery and the excitement of telling someone else about it is still fresh after a good many years. You who have made the same find will know what I mean. We don't always know how to share it, and we sometimes feel very inept in our efforts, but finding Christ brings to all of us an urgent stirring to pass it on. The words of the folk hymn say it well:

> I wish for you, my friends,
> This happiness that I've found.

Philip's friend Nathanael was a bit skeptical at first. His response was, "Can anything good come out of Nazareth?" Nathanael apparently was from Cana, a rival town in Galilee. He wasn't too impressed with what he knew about Nazareth. What could really be expected from a two-bit town like that? That was a natural sort of response, I suppose. We judge everything we hear from the perspective of our own experience; and it is hard for us to believe that anything significant can arise out of familiar surroundings, or especially from a source that we are accustomed to view with contempt. That is probably why a prophet seldom receives honor in his own country, or why the relatives of an outstanding man are sometimes the last ones to see his greatness.

There were many in Jesus' time who were made to stumble by the ordinary situation out of which He came. "Is not this the carpenter's son?" they asked. "Is not his mother called Mary and are not his brothers James and Joseph and Simon and Judas, and are not all his sisters with us? Where then did this man get all this?" Or, "He never went to a school of the rabbis; He never studied theology. How can He do all this teaching?" Or, "He associates with crooks and shysters and women of the streets. What good can you expect from Him?" But the greatest stumbling block of all was the ignominy and shame of His death. The cross was the ultimate scandal. For a person to be hanged on a tree meant death under the curse of the Almighty. How on earth could such a victim be someone to believe in?

Those who attempt today to share what they have found in Christ meet similar objections. In some areas the preaching of the Gospel seems to be associated (in the minds of some at least) with ignorance and superstition. Can anything meaningful for life in the twentieth century come out of that? Many others are disillusioned with the church, weary with its inconsistencies, impatient with its slowness to change. Young people from church families are sometimes alienated by the sham of what they see at home. They cry, "The church — can it have anything worthwhile to give me?"

These are questions not to be lightly dismissed. Often the people asking them are deeply in earnest, searching hard for what life is all about. The way to answer them is not by trying to defend what the church is doing or not doing, or by denying the foibles and failures of those who claim the Christian name. Far better to follow Philip's line. When confronted by Nathaniel's hesitancy and skepticism, Philip didn't respond with excuse or debate. His word was simple and direct — "Come and see."

That's the word I want to bring to you who are not fully convinced about Jesus Christ and His claims. We who have found meaning and life and hope in Jesus Christ say to you, our friends, "This is what we have discovered. We hear your questions and we admit that your criticisms of us are often all too true. We want to take your objections seriously, although we know we can't fully answer them all. Our word to you is one of sincere invitation: 'Come and see.' "

Suppose you are looking through a high-powered microscope at a drop of lake water. You see all kinds of tiny organisms swimming around before your eyes. You try to tell me what you see. But let's say I haven't looked through a microscope before and I haven't heard much about what pollution is doing to our lakes; so I reply to you, "That's all right for you to believe that, but as for myself, I don't really think there's anything swimming around in that drop of water." You could try to argue with me. You could tell me about the latest findings on the number of microorganisms in an average drop of lake water, or you could chide me for doubting your word or suggesting that you have hallucinations, but none of that would help much. The best thing to do is to invite me to come over and look through the microscope myself. If I am willing to give it a try, then the chances are good that I'll see for myself. I won't need your persuasion, your attempts at description any more. If after being invited I'm still reluctant to look through the microscope, you might reason with me this way: "Really, what do you have to lose? If you look and don't see anything there, that will settle it for you and you will be right where you are now. But if you see something new, then we can share it and talk about it and learn together. Why not give it a try? You'll never be sure until you personally look into it."

Sometimes we feel that we'd like to have all our questions answered before we make a deep commitment. "Let's have the mysteries solved, the difficulties cleared up. Then we'll take our stand." But somehow it never works that way. There is always one more thing that isn't quite clear. A point comes when we simply have to act on the basis of the evidence we have if we are to find the truth about Jesus Christ. We have to get up — as it were — from where we are, walk over, and look through that microscope.

That's what Nathanael did. He went along with Philip to find out for himself. When Jesus met him, He called Nathanael a true Israelite, "in whom there is no guile." By that I suppose He meant that Nathanael was willing in spite of his doubts and prejudices to keep on searching for the truth. And that's all the Lord wants from you — an honest openness to Him, a willingness to come and see for yourself. Nathanael later was moved to exclaim, "Rabbi, you are the Son of God." He came and he saw. And Jesus told him that this was only the beginning. "You shall see greater things than these."

There is more you are going to find out about Jesus Christ than what you first discover when you come to Him. Each obedient step in His direction brings further light. The more you open your life to Him, the more fully will He make Himself real to you. Are you willing to take a step toward Him today? To read a passage from the Bible that speaks of Him? To talk to an acquaintance who knows Him? To go to a worship service where His message is told? Or will you right now in a simple prayer tell Him that you are willing to be convinced, that you want to know if He is really God's Son and the Savior of the world? If today you will hear His invitation, "Come and see," and take one step toward Him, you will find Him coming to meet you. And then the great discovery will be yours — to share with someone else.

QUESTIONS FOR DISCUSSION

1. Why do people share their happy discoveries with others?

2. Why is Christian witness of this kind often more effective than theological argument?

3. Why do you suppose that prophets are usually without honor among their own countrymen?

4. Christians are sometimes confronted with a challenge like this: "Prove to me that the Christian faith is true, and then I'll make a commitment." How would you respond to that challenge?

4. A Glimpse of the Glory

When the steward of the feast tasted the water now become wine, and did not know where it came from (though the servants who had drawn the water knew), the steward of the feast called the bridegroom and said to him, "Every man serves the good wine first; and when men have drunk freely, then the poor wine; but you have kept the good wine until now." This, the first of his signs, Jesus did at Cana in Galilee, and manifested his glory; and his disciples believed in him.

(John 2:9-11)

HAVE YOU EVER caught a glimpse of something so supremely attractive that it started you on a search for what you had seen? Maybe it was a wide landscape that promised peace, or a forest waiting to be explored, or a face you couldn't forget. Once you had seen it, a yearning was awakened and you were never quite the same again. In the fascinating allegory *Pilgrim's Regress*, by C. S. Lewis, the hero, John, had an experience like that. He gazed one day into a woodland near his home and heard sweet music. Suddenly he seemed to see, momentarily and far away, a calm sea and an enchanting island. The scene quickened in him such an intense longing that he couldn't rest until he had set out to find that island. One glimpse began a lifelong quest.

If you've ever been in love, you know that there was a moment when you first saw something special in your beloved — the way she smiled, the toss of her head, the way she looked at you. That did it. You were hooked. Or perhaps it was *his* confident way, the laughter in his eyes, the set of his chin, that first attracted you. One word spoken, one moment shared, and you somehow knew that here was the person you had been waiting for.

A life-transforming faith, a conversion, often begins just that way. A moment of vision, then a lifetime of commitment. That's how it was with the first followers of Jesus Christ. As they met Him, listened to Him, watched Him in action, one by one they saw something in Him that moved them profoundly. The Apostle John tells of one incident in particular that made a deep impression on the men who had gathered around Jesus. It happened at a wedding festival in the Galilean town of Cana. The wedding party may well have included Jesus' relatives, since His mother Mary seems to have been active in serving the guests. We don't know exactly why, but soon after the feast began the supply of wine was exhausted. Mary told her Son about the problem, evidently expecting Him to do something about it. Jesus' reply seemed gruff, almost a rebuke: "O woman, what have you to do with me? My hour has not yet come." He seemed to be saying that He had His own destiny to fulfill and could no longer be guided by her wishes. It wasn't long, however, before He told the servants in the household to fill several large stone jars with water. The servants, puzzled but reassured by Mary, did as they were instructed. Later, Jesus told them to draw from those same jars and take the contents to the steward of the feast. The steward was apparently the official "taster" of the wine. He was so delighted with what the servants brought him that he praised the bridegroom highly: "You have kept the good wine until now."

31

In this homely but strange event, John tells us, the first followers of Jesus caught a glimpse of His glory. It wasn't simply that they were amazed at what He did. They somehow became assured by it that God Himself, the Lord of all the universe, was present and active among them in Jesus. That was a remarkable conviction, to say the least. What led them to it? What did they see that convinced them? For one thing, *they saw Him doing what only God can do.* Think of it this way. God is changing water into wine all the time. He sends the rain that refreshes the earth. To the vines on a thousand hills He gives life, and roots to draw moisture from the soil. Then the miracle happens. By God's power the rain from heaven becomes the fruit of the vine; the water becomes wine. In other words, what God does through processes which we call "natural," Jesus does by the mere putting forth of His will. This John calls a "sign," a pointer to something beyond itself. Nature's life-giving Lord has come to dwell among men. Here He is!

The miracle takes place completely without fanfare. We read no announcement of it, not even a description of how it happened. There are no magic words spoken, no wands waved. No one seems to be doing anything — except the servants who go obediently about their task. But the unheard-of thing happens. A transforming power is at work behind the scenes. It is the word and will of Jesus Christ.

"Is that all it took to make them Christians?" someone asks. Men have seen strange things before — and since. Amazement at marvelous happenings does not always lead us to personal faith and commitment. There must have been more here than a prodigy, a wonder. The first disciples of Jesus saw also a hint of how this power at work in Him was to be used. The needs of people were being supplied in a very ordinary situation. This is how God's glory comes to light: *He ministers to the needs of people where they are.*

Sometimes we act as though the Lord's miraculous works are designed only to bring about faith in Him, to endorse His claims. To see it that way is to miss the heartening fact that He wills to do us good, that His power is put forth for *us*. Jesus came to reveal God's glory among men, but He never performed miracles just to demonstrate who He was; in fact, He resisted the temptation to put on that kind of performance. He came to use His life-giving, transforming power for people. Having the power to heal, He could not do otherwise, regardless of the effect which His miracles might have on those who witnessed them. They were acts of love as well as displays of power. He cared about people in their sicknesses and embarrassments, their wants and frustrations, their longings and sins.

A poet writes poems not to become famous, but because he is a poet. The fame comes later when people recognize the poetry that issues from within the man. And so it was with Christ's glory — the glory of self-giving love. It was precisely because His first followers saw in Him this caring for others, this ministering to the everyday needs of men, that they could discern who He really was.

But the most evident factor in this scene is *Jesus' concern for human joy*. Imagine — God providing the wine at a wedding celebration! Most of us aren't accustomed to thinking of God in that light. We know Him as law-maker, taskmaster, and ruler. We can think of Him also as Savior and giver of gifts; but it is less often, it seems to me, that we think of Him as joy-bringer.

This aspect of His ministry may have taken Jesus' first followers by surprise. Some of them had admired the austere life of John the Baptist; and they perhaps believed that Jesus, too, would be a recluse, a man of the desert, far from places of feasting and merriment. If He was indeed the Son of God from heaven, surely He would have little time for the joys of earth! And what would the King of Israel have to do with the wine supply at a common family festival? During Jesus' lifetime many were scandalized at His easy familiarity with all kinds of people and at His freedom in joining their celebrations. Many of us have the same problem now. We are hardly ready — even in our churches — for the God who laughs and wants us to laugh.

Maybe it's for that reason — because we have such difficulty in keeping joy and religion together — that Christ chose to reveal His glory first at a marriage feast: not in a temple or synagogue, not even at a retreat or a prayer meeting, but at one of the happy moments of our common life.

He comes to redeem all of life for us. In Him we see, not contempt for human feelings but sharing in them, not a separation from human sympathies but a deepening and enriching of them. He comes honoring all our joys, renewing all relationship, hallowing all occasions. He is no aloof spectator—God, but one who comes to enter our lives and complete our joy. No one can live in the presence of Jesus Christ and still think of God as a kill-joy or a bore. We may spoil our joys with excess or pollute them with selfishness, and certainly He has no part in that. But never forget it: He is on the side of gladness.

Do we want to be holy, God-like? Then we cannot be apostles of gloom. Otherworldliness, if that means despising earthly joys and viewing the lighthearted with contempt, is surely not the way of Christ. To follow Him is to be genuinely and intensely human. However difficult and demanding the path of obedience may be, it is a way of singing and gladness.

Yet the joy which Christ brings, though never alien to our common joys, is richer and deeper than they. It is full of new surprises. Without Him, our joys, like the wine of the feast, are soon exhausted. The law of diminishing returns seems to operate in most human satisfactions. The first taste is most delightful; the second is almost as good; but after that, nothing quite measures up. That's why the joys we have known seem incomplete when once we find Him. There is a better gift, a higher happiness. There is a fountain of joy that never runs dry. As the psalmist put it, "in thy presence there is fulness of joy, in thy right hand are pleasures for evermore" (Ps. 16:11). Christians sing, "Sweeter as the years go by," and they mean it. Christ keeps the best until last.

None of those witnesses at the wedding understood all that was involved in what Jesus did there. They had only a fleeting glimpse of His purpose to bring new life and happiness to the world. They knew little of how costly it would be, how dark a path He would tread to bring them gladness. But Jesus Himself must have seen far more in what He did at Cana than domestic helpfulness. Wine stands for gladness; but for Him at a deeper level it was to stand for blood, for a poured-out life. As He put forth His power to restore the joy of these wedding guests, He must have been reminded that His own life would one day be poured out for the renewal of many. The "hour" in which He ministers to this simple need points to that greater hour when He will give Himself for the deepest wants of men. With Him nothing is trivial, because the same love that leads Him to fulfill each common joy will at last go through death so that we may taste the joy of forgiveness and find a purity that washings and ceremonies could never give.

So if those first disciples could see Jesus' glory in that wedding feast, how much more shall we? If they believed because they saw Him furnish wedding guests with wine, how much more shall we believe who know that for centuries He has furnished the broken-hearted with comfort, the despairing with hope, the guilty with forgiveness, and every searching heart with the glad knowledge of God Himself?

It may not all become clear for us at once, any more than it did for them; but wherever we see the transforming power of Christ at work, doing what only God can do, wherever we see Him meeting the needs of people, crowning them with His greater joy, there we catch sight of His glory. And then the lifelong quest begins.

Has it begun for you? Have you seen in Christ something supremely attractive, uniquely worthy? Then you are on the way. The next step is to commit as much as you know of yourself to as much as you know of God in Christ. Obey that vision now. Don't wait until everything becomes fully clear. Act on what you see. It gets clearer — and better — as you go along. He will make your joy full and lasting. He will even make you a joy-bringer to the world.

QUESTIONS FOR DISCUSSION

1. Why and how did you first experience "a glimpse of the glory"? Share that with your group.

2. What are some of the things done for people by Jesus "which only God could do"?

3. In what loving actions of other people have you been most aware of Christ's presence?

4. What, in your opinion, are the greatest hindrances to joy in the lives of religious people?

5. What Nice People Need

Now there was a man of the Pharisees, named Nico-
demus, a ruler of the Jews. This man came to Jesus by
night and said to him, "Rabbi, we know that you are a
teacher come from God; for no one can do these signs
that you do, unless God is with him." Jesus answered
him, "Truly, truly, I say to you, unless one is born
anew, he cannot see the kingdom of God."

(John 3:1-3)

JESUS CHRIST WAS often very blunt with people. You
might say that His public relations methods were not in
the best modern tradition! It wasn't simply that He
told hard-hearted religionists that they were hypocrites,
whitewashed tombs, and blind leaders of the blind. He
even seemed to discourage promising candidates for
discipleship. One day an eager volunteer approached
Him and said, "I will follow you wherever you go."
Instead of welcoming him with open arms, Jesus threw
cold water on the whole project by saying, "Foxes have
holes, and birds of the air have nests; but the Son of
man has nowhere to lay his head" (Matt. 8:20). Another young rich man with a fine record came respect-
fully to ask an important question. "Good Master, what
shall I do to inherit eternal life?" Jesus' reply must
have been a shocker: "Why do you call Me good? No

one is good but God alone. You know the commandments." He went on to make the way of discipleship so demanding that the young man turned away, shaking his head sadly. And Jesus didn't urge him or call him back. He simply let him go.

But perhaps the most brusque and surprising of all His interviews with people was the one with Nicodemus. This man was a Pharisee, deeply concerned about his religion. He was a ruler of the Jews, holding a highly responsible position in the Sanhedrin. Unlike many of his colleagues, however, he seemed to be favorably disposed toward Jesus. See how courteous and friendly he was in his opening words: "Rabbi, we know that you are a teacher come from God; for no one can do these signs that you do, unless God is with him." Nicodemus, an older man, well schooled in the Jewish faith, recognized the unlettered Jesus as a rabbi. More than that, he saw Him as a divinely authorized teacher. He looked at Jesus' miracles not skeptically or critically, but saw them as signs that God was with this new teacher. Most men would have been highly flattered by this sort of visit and by these expressions of confidence and esteem. Nicodemus was certainly holding out the olive branch. He seems to have been a man of generous spirit. Imagine his dismay when Jesus answered, "Truly, truly, I say to you, unless one is born anew, he cannot see the kingdom of God." If any of Jesus' followers were present, they must have winced at this. "Lord, don't You know who this man is? Shouldn't You use a little more tact?" The abruptness of His words still grates on us today. The plain truth is that Jesus seems at times to have offended people whom most modern clergymen could easily have enrolled in the church!

However gracious the words of Nicodemus seem to us, they did not impress Jesus. He not only declined to acknowledge the compliment, but He turned things around by calling into question the visitor's whole religious outlook. Nicodemus spoke about God with easy confidence: "We know that you are a teacher come from God." Jesus questioned whether he had ever really seen God's kingdom. Nicodemus talked as a man experienced in divine things, but Jesus told him that he needed a new beginning in his life. He must be born again!

Here, apparently, is what all people — even nice people — need. And now I speak especially to you who can identify in some way with Nicodemus: religious people, fair-minded people, those willing to allow that Christianity has some truth in it, those who esteem Jesus highly as an inspired teacher. I speak to pleasant, cultivated people who wish every good cause well; and I say, listen intently to this strange word of Jesus Christ: "You must be born anew."

That famous preacher of the eighteenth century, George Whitefield, once wrote these words to Benjamin Franklin: "My dear sir, I find you grow more and more famous in the learned world. As you have made a pretty considerable progress in the mysteries of electricity, I would now honestly recommend to your diligent, unprejudiced pursuit and study the mysteries of the new birth." There is a good word for us. Let's inquire into those mysteries together. And let our first question be this one: Why is a new birth *necessary?* Why this absolute prerequisite for entering into God's kingdom? Jesus deals with that question in these words: "That which is born of the flesh is flesh, and that which is born of the Spirit is spirit." In other words, to see God's kingdom and enter into it, a new kind of life is needed — a life which we human beings are powerless to produce. Human nature can beget only human nature, nothing more; and that is not enough.

Here is a crucial point in Jesus' understanding of man. In the passage immediately before this one, we learn that many believed in Jesus' name when they saw the signs which He did, but "Jesus did not trust himself to them because he knew all men and needed no one to bear witness of man, for he himself knew what was in man." Jesus Christ knows what is in the human heart, and on the basis of that knowledge He insists that each of us must be radically renewed if he is to live in God's presence.

At this point a host of people are ready to object. Every other great world religion assumes that man is perfectible. He may have flaws, he may have evil qualities about him, but he can change his situation. By his good conduct, by his godward aspirations, by his spiritual disciplines he can bridge the gap between his humanness and the divine glory. But the Christian view is different. Here the gulf is too wide to be bridged by human effort. The problem is too deep for self-improvement. In our hearts, in our inmost being, we are rebels against the God who made us. Created to love God and love our fellow men, we are curved in upon ourselves. We make ourselves the center of life. We go our own way, rather than God's way. It is not simply that our actions are imperfect; the whole direction of our life is wrong. The stream is polluted at the source and carries the taint wherever it goes. No patchwork, no superficial remedies can possibly help. We need a radical change if we are to live with the God who is light and in whom there is no darkness at all.

We sometimes try to evade this indictment by comparing ourselves favorably with others. "This picture of human life may be true for criminals, tyrants, and child molesters," we acknowledge, "but certainly not for me." But that is to deny the humanity we share with everyone else. And that won't do. The seeds of the worst things are in the best of us. That, at least, is how Christ viewed all men. In speaking to Nicodemus, He likened our spiritual plight to that of the Israelites in the desert when many of them were bitten by poisonous snakes. A malady with fatal effects has seized upon all of us. That's why we need a new birth.

Well now, assuming that such a thing is necessary, how is it *possible?* That was what baffled Nicodemus. "How can a man be born when he is old?" he asked. "Can he enter a second time into his mother's womb and be born?" The question is less naive than it sounds. Nicodemus must have known that Jesus wasn't referring to another physical birth. A deeper question haunts his wistful response. How can a man have a genuinely new beginning? Isn't everyone the sum of all his yesterdays? Doesn't the past shape us inexorably and determine what we are? It would be wonderful to break free from it, to have a fresh start; but how is that possible?

Jesus' answer, as we have seen, excludes every human possibility. The words *born anew* can also be translated *born from above,* and that double meaning is probably intended. Rebirth is quickened by nothing on earth, but only by God Himself. The new life must come from heaven. We must be born of the Spirit. Jesus goes on to say that this new birth is made possible by God's love. We human beings can neither produce nor deserve it. It comes as sheer gift because God cares for us. He wants us to have a new beginning. He wants us to live with Him.

But His love is more than a wish, more than a sentiment. It has gone into action on our behalf. "God so loved the world that he gave his only Son." The specific event that makes a new birth possible is the gift of Christ, the lifting up of the Son of man. Jesus is to be lifted up on a cross. He is to suffer there in our stead, bearing away the sins of the world. Once crucified, He will rise again to give new life to the world. Men and women can be born of the Spirit as this risen Christ comes to live in their hearts, quickening, transforming, making all things new. Here is God's solution to our need: the love of the Father, the sacrifice of the Son, and the life-giving power of the Spirit.

Now, for one more question: If the new birth is necessary and possible, how can it be *experienced?* If it is indeed God's own work, as sovereign, free, and unpredictable as the wind, if you can't get yourself born again by any human means, must you simply wait in hope for a divine miracle? Must you wait until the Spirit "hits you," until some power from the outside turns your life around? No, Christ has shown us how the new life, God's gift of love, can be received. Look again at that strange scene from Israel's wilderness wanderings. The people, prone to murmur and complain against God, have been bitten by poisonous snakes. Moses cries to God on their behalf, "Lord, what shall we do?" The remedy proposed was unusual, to say the least. Moses was to make a serpent, a snake, out of brass and set it high on a pole in the midst of the encampment. God promised that any of the stricken Israelites who would look at the brazen serpent would survive. Now, Jesus takes that obscure incident, remembered in only a few lines of the Old Testament, and fills it with new meaning. "As Moses lifted up the serpent in the wilderness, so must the Son of man be lifted up, that whoever believes in him may have eternal life."

Do you see the parallel? Bitten by serpents, poisoned by sin; the hope of healing, the promise of new life; a serpent on a pole, a Savior on a cross. And now for the crucial point of the parallel: looking toward the promised remedy is a picture of what it means to believe in Jesus Christ. When a dying victim heard of God's provision and inched his way to the tent door to catch a glimpse of God's cure, he was exercising faith. And when we who know our personal need, our helplessness to save ourselves, look toward Christ as one dying in our place, we find life — the life that is life indeed.

Charles Spurgeon, the remarkable English preacher of the last century, first experienced God's transforming power in his life when a lay minister of very limited abilities simply repeated over and over again the verse, "Look unto me and be saved, all the ends of the earth."

Look! Look! That may seem absurdly simple to you, as perhaps it did to Nicodemus. And looking at a serpent on a pole may have seemed ridiculous to many who stayed in their tents — and died there. But millions of people — the nice and the not-so-nice, the cultured and the boorish, religious and profane — will testify that looking toward Christ, trusting the crucified and risen Lord, has made all things new for them. Jesus says to you and to me, as He did to Nicodemus, "You must be born anew." Don't be put off by that startling demand. Behind it is a heart of love that knows what even nice people need. And what Jesus demands, He offers. There is life in a look at the Savior.

QUESTIONS FOR DISCUSSION

1. How do you understand Jesus' rather abrupt manner with Nicodemus, and with some who volunteered to be His disciples?

2. How would you explain to a cultured, personable acquaintance his need for a new birth?

3. In what sense does the new birth of which Jesus speaks make us different? Will our personalities be radically altered? Discuss this.

4. Faith is often referred to in the Bible as a kind of "looking" or "seeing." How do these actions picture what it means to believe?

6. What Naughty People Want

There came a woman of Samaria to draw water. Jesus said to her, "Give me a drink." For his disciples had gone away into the city to buy food. The Samaritan woman said to him, "How is it that you, a Jew, ask a drink of me, a woman of Samaria?" For Jews have no dealings with Samaritans. Jesus answered her, "If you knew the gift of God, and who it is that is saying to you, 'Give me a drink,' you would have asked him and he would have given you living water."

(John 4:7-10)

WE WERE THINKING in the previous chapter of how sharply Jesus Christ sometimes spoke to nice people, how He brought them up short by confronting them with their need. Today we watch Him dealing with a different kind of person — the kind that nice people shake their heads over and whisper about. These are the naughty, the not-so-nice, those whose faults and failings make up the stuff of common gossip. With them we find Christ strangely gentle. For them He has no stern imperatives. He seems rather to aim at helping them find what they most deeply want.

Jesus is sitting by a well on the outskirts of a Samaritan village when a woman comes there to draw water. Contrary to custom and popular prejudice, He asks her for a drink. Bitter animosity rankled between Jews and Samaritans in those days, and no conscientious Jews would have thought of drinking from a vessel provided by a Samaritan. But Jesus ignores that social barrier to ask a simple favor. The woman responds with surprise — and with some suspicion. "How is it that you, a Jew, ask a drink of me, a woman of Samaria?" She seems to say, "We both know how it is between Jews and Samaritans. Why then should You ask a favor of me, and why should I do anything for You?"

In reply Jesus simply turns His attention to what the woman wants. "If you knew the gift of God and who it is that is saying to you, 'Give me a drink,' you would have asked him, and he would have given you living water." If she had only realized who He was and what He came to give, she herself would have broken the social code to ask for something. She doubts, however, that He has anything to give. With a touch of scorn she answers, "Sir, you have nothing to draw with and the well is deep; where do you get that living water? Are you greater than our father Jacob, who gave us the well?" "Really, who do You think you are?" Not put off by her taunts, Jesus goes on speaking about her — about what she deeply longs for. "You've come here for water," He says. "Every one who drinks of this water will thirst again, but whoever drinks of the water I shall give him will never thirst; the water that I shall give him will become in him a spring of water welling up to eternal life."

What human heart wouldn't respond to that? We all crave satisfaction and fulfillment. The human spirit knows a thirst of which the body's craving for water is a sign. But the satisfaction we inwardly crave always seems to elude us. We grasp for it, we almost have it, and then it vanishes again. The old thirst comes back, stronger than ever. Who wouldn't want a satisfaction that abides — a fountain of refreshment that keeps springing up? Isn't that what people are after today in their search for thrills and kicks? Doesn't this set many of us on the merry-go-round of pleasure seeking — let's try one drink, one drug, one delight after another in the hope that somewhere we'll be satisfied? In the case of some, like the Samaritan woman, it was one partner after another, one home after another, always hoping, always questing for a happiness that lasts, but never finding it.

Does that speak to you today? To a restlessness within you? A clamoring thirst of the heart that nothing can seem to quiet? Has it led you, perhaps, into paths that have turned out to be dead ends? Into ways of living that make you uncomfortable to remember? How many of the follies and evils into which all of us fall come from the yearnings we try so hard to satisfy!

But here is someone promising living water, a refreshment that never runs dry. Even this cautious woman, so often burned by false promises, shows interest. For the first time she is ready to ask for something. "Sir, give me this water, that I may not thirst, nor come here to draw." "By all means," she is saying, "if You can really provide what You are talking about, please give me it! Heaven knows how long I've been searching!"

Now the conversation takes a turn. Jesus said, "Go, call your husband, and come here." We can almost sense the pained silence that followed. Jesus had touched a sensitive spot. "I have no husband," she answered. "You are right in saying, 'I have no husband,'" said Jesus, "for you have had five husbands, and he whom you now have is not your husband; this you said truly." What a moment that was! Jesus affirmed her answer and then went on to show that He knew all about her domestic problems. It must have been a frightening disclosure. Here was a man of another country, whom she had never seen before, who could recount in detail the record of her past. This was too much to take! With quick nervousness, she changed the subject. "Since You are a prophet with such powers, tell me the answer to this controversial issue. Which is the proper place for worship, Mount Gerizim or Jerusalem?" Now there was a fine matter for discussion! One could debate it for hours without becoming too personally involved. Anything to get off the subject of five husbands — and a present companion of doubtful status!

But this insight of Jesus into her marital history had made a profound impression on the woman. She later spoke of it as the most remarkable thing about her encounter with Him. It wasn't simply that He knew about her; all of that was probably common talk in the village where she lived. And it wasn't merely the unusual twist that a stranger should know all this. It was the rest of the conversation that made this one feature of it so impressive. Here was someone who did not condemn or ridicule her because of what He knew. His comment on her past came out kindly, in connection with an offer of living water, lasting satisfaction. In other words, He was providing something else that she really wanted: acceptance.

We all want that, don't we? Give us someone who knows us through and through and yet accepts us just as we are. We're all too familiar, as this woman must have been, with what only *seems* to be acceptance. People welcome us for what we can do for them. They shower us with gifts and attention so as the better to exploit us. And we know about conditional acceptance, too. Some are friendly until they get to know about us, until they discover that we've made some mistakes. Then they grow cool. Others promise to befriend us if we'll only change and become like them, or like they want us to be. "When you get over all your bad habits," they seem to say, "then we'll want you around." But how rare a thing it is when people know us, "warts and all," and still take us to their hearts! That is acceptance.

And that was what this woman felt in Jesus' presence. Here was a man who had asked her a favor. He wanted to be served by her. He had put up with her crossness, her sharp tongue, her ill-disguised mocking, and had offered her a happiness she hardly dared to hope for. And all the while He had known what kind of woman she was! She found that strange — and profoundly moving. People always do, especially if they have felt the lash of scorn or known the loneliness that ostracism and contempt can bring. Everyone longs for acceptance, but none can feel the need of it quite as keenly as the despised, the talked-about and the looked-down-on. The woman who is twice divorced, the teenager with a police record, the alcoholic, the mentally ill, the businessman who has gone through bankruptcy — they know how important it is (and how rare) to be accepted.

This woman of Samaria had known more than her share of nonacceptance. She probably came to the well at an odd time of day to avoid the smirks and taunts of other women in her community. In her conversation with Jesus she encountered a new kind of love, the tough acceptance that confronts us with what we've done and makes us come to terms with it, but then welcomes us to a future bright with hope.

But now back to the conversation at the well. The woman may have tried to sidetrack Jesus with her question about the proper place for worship, but still He took it seriously. He let her know that *how* people worship is more significant than *where*. God seeks a worship from transformed hearts, based on the truth which He reveals. A new day for the worship of God's people is dawning before this woman's eyes. God is here now — not in a temple or on a mountain, but in the person of Jesus. Still she fails to understand. Her ideas of worship are confused. Her questions about the meaning of religion still wait for an answer. Wistfully she looks ahead. "I know that Messiah is coming:

when he comes, he will show us all things." Here again she voices a longing common to many. "Oh, to find certainty in my complex, controversial questions about religion! Where is someone who can clear up these things once and for all? If only the Messiah, the promised one, would come!" At that Jesus directs her attention again to Himself. "I who speak to you am he."

The conversation ends right there. All her questions are not answered, but what she has learned is far more significant. In C. S. Lewis's book, *Till We Have Faces,* Queen Orual complains bitterly against the gods — until she meets the true Lord. Then her attitude changes. "I ended my book with the words, 'No answer.' I know now, Lord, why you utter no answer. You are yourself the answer. Before your face questions die away. What other answer would suffice?" The queen was satisfied, and so was this woman of Samaria. She forgot about what she came for, dropped her water pot by the well, and ran back to the village to spread the news.

Now many of you may feel some kinship with this obscure woman of the past. These words may be especially for you. You are not particularly religious, perhaps. You're ready to admit that some things in your life have not been what they should be. You've known what it is to be criticized, to feel rejected. You search for happiness in life, for genuine accepting love, for an answer to your deepest questions. Let me assure you today that Jesus Christ is interested in you, and that He has something for you. He meets you, too, in the common circumstances of your life and tells you that living water is yours for the asking. And as you take Him seriously, as you get to know Him, you discover that all you've been most deeply wanting is there — in Him. He, in person, dying for you and rising again, is God's acceptance, God's welcome. The new life He gives can slake every thirst, and the truth you find in Him is the answer you are seeking. Jesus is both the Savior we need and the satisfaction we want.

Arnold Toynbee, perhaps the greatest historian of our time, put it well when he said, "As we, in this our time of troubles, await on the banks of Time's river in anguished longing for a deliverer, a single figure arises from the flood and straightway fills the whole horizon. There is the Savior and the pleasure of the Lord shall prosper in his land. He shall see the travail of his soul and be satisfied." Yes, and so will we if we stretch out toward Him the empty cup of faith and take the living water!

QUESTIONS FOR DISCUSSION

1. What does Jesus' ministry at the well teach us about breaking down social barriers?

2. What are the steps by which Jesus led this woman to faith in Himself?

3. What can we learn from this interview about dealing with the questions and objections of inquirers?

4. What are some of the fundamental human needs which find fulfillment in Christ?

7. Why Some People Stay Away

You search the scriptures, because you think that in them you have eternal life; and it is they that bear witness to me; yet you refuse to come to me that you may have life. How can you believe, who receive glory from one another and do not seek the glory that comes from the only God?

(John 5:39, 40, 44)

WHY DO SOME people stay away from Christ? Many, of course, do not believe because the good news has never been brought to them. This we can understand. As the Apostle Paul put it, "How are they to believe in him of whom they have never heard? And how are they to hear without a preacher?" (Rom. 10:14). But what of those who have heard and still do not believe? How do we account for that? Why, for example, did many of Jesus' contemporaries not become His followers? Why were they cool toward Him? Why could some not bear to have Him around? Or, to bring it closer to home, why have some of your friends and relatives not become Christians? Or perhaps the question applies directly to you. If you are not a Christian, why is that? Perhaps you have heard the message of Christ many times. You're a reasonably religious person, concerned about doing the right thing. But up until now you have stayed away from personal commitment to Christ. Why?

Before you answer that, let me point out what Jesus Himself had to say about it. He was addressing a group of people who did not believe. In fact, they were actively opposing Him. It seems that Jesus had completely healed a paralyzed man. What made the event so remarkable was the fact that the man had been helpless for some thirty-eight years. But some of the religious leaders were deeply disturbed that this work of healing had been done on the sabbath day. When they challenged Him, however, He made no apologies. His answer came back bold and startling, "My Father is working still, and I am working." Here Jesus calls God "My Father" and identifies His work with God's. His opponents were quick to recognize what He meant. From this point on they were even more determined to do away with Him because in their eyes, as John writes, "He not only broke the sabbath but also called God his own father, making himself equal with God."

And this, after all, is the central Christian claim, isn't it — that Jesus Christ is God's own Son, one with the Father? Here were people who heard it from His lips and called it blasphemy. How did Jesus respond to them? To the charge that He was making Himself equal with God, He answered that He wasn't making Himself anything. "Truly, truly I say to you, the Son can do nothing of his own accord, but only what he sees the father doing." All that he has, in other words, is because of the Father's gift. All that He does, springs from the Father's work. The Father has put everything in His hands so that all may honor Him even as they honor the Father. In fact, He insists that no one can really honor God who does not honor Jesus as God's Son. Pause a minute over that. All the honor, reverence, worship, and obedience that we owe to Almighty God we owe to Jesus Christ. What an astounding claim! It is either the biggest lie or the best news ever told. Can it stand up? Is it believable?

Jesus tells His hearer that the evidence for it is all around them. For example, they had considered John the Baptist quite a prophet. Had not John borne his witness to Jesus as God's Son? And what about all those works of healing and mercy? Surely they testified that the Father had sent Him. Jesus goes on to claim that the Old Testament Scriptures, long cherished and pored over by God's people, bear witness to Him. "You search the scriptures," He says, "because you think that in them you have eternal life; and it is they that bear witness to me."

Why then do these people not believe Him? Because they do not want to. Jesus says it bluntly: "You refuse to come to me that you may have life." A literal translation of those words would be, "you do not *will* to come to me." Jesus locates the root cause of unbelief in the human will. In other words, when Christ's Gospel is presented to us and we do not respond in faith, the responsibility for that rests squarely with us.

We find that a hard saying, don't we? It's more comfortable to put the responsibility somewhere else. Some say that God is accountable for their unbelief. "The Spirit has never moved me," they protest. "I'm certainly willing to believe, but God just hasn't shown me yet." Or, "Maybe Christianity is just not for me. Maybe I'm not one of the elect." Many pastors talk to people who, consciously or not, express this feeling. When urged to believe, they insist that they can't.

Dietrich Bonhoeffer, in his book *The Call to Discipleship,* says that this is the pastor's moment of opportunity. He isn't to throw up his hands, as though helpless before the mystery of a far-off divine decree. If the responsibility is all God's, if He simply gives faith to some and withholds it from others, the pastor has little to say to the man before him. But Bonhoeffer says it's time to take the bull by the horns with this word: "Only those who obey, believe." That places the responsibility where it belongs. The pastor can then go on to say, "You are disobedient; you are trying to keep some part of your life under your own control. That is what prevents you from listening to Christ and believing in His grace. You cannot hear Christ because you are willfully disobedient. Somewhere in your heart you are refusing to listen to His call."

Others who deny their own responsibility say that the powers of evil are to blame. They echo Flip Wilson's phrase, "The devil made me do it." That ploy is as old as the Garden of Eden. We still like to picture ourselves as the innocent victims of forces beyond our control. That gets us off the hook.

Now the Bible does speak, of course, about the freeness and sovereignty of God's loving approach to men. It does indicate that faith is His gift, and not something we can manufacture within ourselves. It also teaches that the god of this world, the prince of evil, has blinded the minds of those who do not believe. But all this is never taught so as to rule out our primary responsibility. No one is compelled to reject the Gospel. This we do ourselves. Passing the buck won't work; it stops here.

There are others who decline to believe in Christ without appealing to any supernatural cause. They say it makes no sense to them, that other views of life are more plausible. Or they claim to be turned off, offended by some who profess faith in Christ. On their view the evidence is simply not sufficient. They see no particular reason why they *should* believe, since they are not convinced that the Christian faith is true. They think of themselves as sensible people, open to truth, as interested observers, ready to listen to reason. But Christianity hasn't vitally commended itself to them. That's why they don't believe.

But Christ would not let people off with that. His coming, He insisted, brings about a crisis in the lives of men. His hearers are not dealing with just one more set of religious teachings; they are confronting God in person. When people saw what He did and heard what He said they could not be neutral. Their answer couldn't be academic — true or false. It was yes or no to Him. They were either for Him or against Him. They either wanted Him or shunned Him. They willed to follow or they refused. And it is still the same. "You do not will to come to me," He said, "that you might have life."

But the agonizing question persists, Why would people refuse? Why would they not want to come to Christ? Here is a life of incomparable quality. Here is the chief exemplar of the highest we know — self-giving love. Here is one who poured His life out in a caring ministry to the needs of people. He spoke truth — fearlessly, compassionately. If anyone in all the history of the world is worthy to be believed and followed, surely it is Jesus Christ. Those who know and love this Lord find it terribly hard to understand why anyone would want to stay away from Him. What is it that makes coming to Christ so difficult for some?

Listen again to these words of Jesus, "You refuse to come to me that you may have life." What He is saying is this: to come to Him in genuine faith we must acknowledge that in ourselves we have no true life. And some find that desperately hard to admit. Think of these religious leaders, contemporaries of Jesus. They had a glorious heritage. As the Apostle Paul put it, to them belonged "the sonship, the glory, covenants, the giving of the law, the worship and the promises" (Rom. 9:4). They had the law, the Old Testament Scriptures. They were confident that in possessing, studying, honoring those ancient writings they were spiritually alive. But now Jesus tells them that He is the central content of those Scriptures and that only through coming to Him will they find God's life. "What? You mean that all my knowledge, all my sabbath observance, all my law-keeping doesn't count for anything? Is my background, my self-discipline, my religious zeal all for nothing?"

That's the heart of the human problem. We want to be something on our own, apart from the God who gives us life. We want to make a name for ourselves. The searching question of Jesus applies to all of us: "How can you believe, who receive glory from one another and do not seek that glory that comes from the only God?" We flee from God's verdict about our lives. We want to prove to ourselves and to others that we are really something on our own. That's the difficulty, the scandal, in coming to Christ. To believe in Him as a life-giver means to acknowledge our lifelessness, our estrangement from the God who is life. To come to Him for healing is an admission that we are inwardly sick. To seek His forgiveness means confessing our guilt. To come to the light means to be revealed for what we really are.

Actually, the realistic picture of our condition appears earlier in this chapter where Jesus meets the paralytic by the pool. This man has been infirm for a long time. He has sought various means of healing, but all without success. Powerless to change his condition, he has waited in vain for help. No man can meet his need. To him Jesus says, "Do you want to be healed?" There is the same Greek word we noted before. Literally, "Do you *will* to be healed?" That profound question searches us. Are we willing to be made whole?

The person who knows the depth of his need is ready to say yes. The smugly complacent will not. That's why Jesus said to stuffy, self-righteous people in His day, "The tax collectors and the harlots go into the kingdom of God before you" (Matt. 21:31). Not because God is partial to people of that sort, but because they are willing at least to admit their need. When Jesus was criticized for mingling with these despised ones, His response was simply this: "Those who are well have no need of a physician, but those who are sick. I have not come to call the righteous, but sinners to repentance" (Luke 5:31, 32).

Are you willing to see yourself as a sick one in need of healing? A sinner who must repent? A wanderer coming back home? Then you will have no trouble believing. Jesus Christ redeems people like you. But remember — He saves those who know they need saving and who come believingly to Him. When we renounce all trust in what we've done and stop playing God on our own, we find in Christ the life that is life indeed. Why stay away? You need not. God's love longs over you. Christ offers His healing and new life to you. The Spirit and the Lord's people say, "Come, take the water of life freely." But the question is yours personally to answer. "Are you willing to be made whole?"

QUESTIONS FOR DISCUSSION

1. What are some of the explanations or excuses for unbelief which you have heard?

2. How would you counsel a person who says: "I want to believe in Christ, but I can't"?

3. In what sense does the word of Christ produce a *crisis* in the lives of those who hear it?

4. Why do you suppose people like the Pharisees found it hard to believe in Christ?

8. How to Come Alive

So Jesus said to them, "Truly, truly, I say to you, unless you eat the flesh of the Son of man and drink his blood, you have no life in you; he who eats my flesh and drinks my blood has eternal life, and I will raise him up at the last day. For my flesh is food indeed, and my blood is drink indeed. He who eats my flesh and drinks my blood abides in me, and I in him."

(John 6:53-56)

TWO MEN, ONE a friend of mine, stood outside a lavish country estate. They had come to do some repair work on one of the buildings. Quite a scene greeted them. Here was a huge colonial mansion with three gleaming, late-model cars in the garage. Near it were tennis courts, a swimming pool, a stable for horses, and all around — acres of rolling lawn. One man shook his head with a low whistle, "Man, that's the life!" he said. "No," answered my friend, "Jesus Christ is the life." Which do you think was right?

Both of these men were talking about something more than physical existence. They were speaking of a quality of life — what makes for real living. Both implied what all of us deeply feel: there is more to life than bodily survival. People are said to be "alive" or "dead" in a number of ways, aren't they? We often speak of a sound sleeper, for example, as being "dead to the world." He is alive, but he makes no response to what goes on around him. Bright lights, music, persistent prodding — none of these rouse him. He seems, at least for the time being, dead to the world of sense experience.

Once I stood in a long ward at Mercy Hospital in Chicago. Across the aisle from the man I was visiting lay a patient who had been struck on the head some months before by a swinging steel beam. He was breathing; he seemed very much alive, but his eyes were fixed in a vacant stare. No glimmer of consciousness, no light of recognition would ever again brighten his face. He was dead to the world of the mind. Alive, yet not really living. Could that also be said of some who are physically alert and mentally keen? Can personalities that seem vibrant and vital remain, at a deeper level, lifeless? Dead to the world of the Spirit? That is the verdict of Jesus. Listen to this startling statement of His. "Truly, truly, I say to you, unless you eat the flesh of the Son of man and drink his blood, you have no life in you." Think of that! He says that without Him we have no life in us. What can He mean?

Well, in the thought world of the Bible, God is seen as the source and giver of life — physical vitality, mental acumen, and also life at a more profound level. This deeper kind of life is meant for mankind alone. Only of the human creation was it said, "God . . . breathed into his nostrils the breath of life; and man became a living being" (Gen. 2:7). Among all of God's creative works, we human beings are unique. We alone are made in God's image, for a special relationship with Him. This is our true humanness. We are made for God, for a mutual relationship of loyalty and love. In that fellowship with the life-giver, we find our life.

But when the bond of harmony between creator and creature is broken, life ebbs away. We broke that bond. We chose to go our own way, to declare our independence of God. And we found His word of warning to be true: "In the day you eat of it you shall die" (Gen. 2:17). Not that we experience physical death the moment we first disobey God. That rarely happens to anyone. But something within all of us *has* died. The vital bond that links us to our maker and Lord has been severed. We are like branches newly broken from a tree. The leaves still appear green and supple, the wood healthy and firm, but the forces of death are already at work. The branch no longer cleaves to its source of life. Away from God, we are like cut flowers, keeping our borrowed beauty for awhile but destined soon to fade and wither. Here is the ultimate tragedy of our history — that we are cut off, separated from our creator and life-giver. We have lost our true life.

Yes, and Jesus Christ makes the daring claim that we will never find it again apart from Him. That's the significance of those words about life with which He repeatedly describes Himself. He is the bread of life. He imparts the water of life. He provides the light of life. He is, Himself, the life eternal. And He came to earth that we might have that life — abundantly.

But there is more to His claim even than that. Jesus tells His hearers that their hope of life is linked with His flesh and blood. "Unless you eat the flesh of the Son of man and drink his blood, you have no life in you." A remarkable expression! It means, among other things, the separation of His flesh from His blood. That seems to point toward the very opposite of life — toward death.

Remember Shylock, in Shakespeare's play, *The Merchant of Venice?* He was the villain who demanded a grisly sort of payment if a certain obligation wasn't honored. He insisted on a pound of his debtor's flesh. When the score wasn't settled, things looked bad for the debtor. But the clever judge in this case foiled Shylock by ruling that he could take the pound of flesh from his victim, but if in doing so he shed one drop of *blood* his own life would be forfeit. That separation, of course, was impossible. Flesh and blood cling together in every living man or woman. When they are torn apart in us, we are beginning to die.

That is the meaning beneath the surface here. When Jesus says that we have no life apart from His flesh and blood, He speaks of the death He is about to die. It is to be a self-offering for others, a sacrifice for the sins of the world. On that, He maintains, the life of the world will depend.

Here is what some people find hard to accept in the Christian faith. "Do you mean that we are dependent for true life, not only upon this person, Jesus Christ, but upon His actually dying a violent death?" Many in our Lord's time were offended at the thought. One who died as a condemned man, especially on a cross, was thought to be accursed of God. The death of Christ proved at times to be a serious stumbling block for would-be followers. It was hard even for His disciples to take in. When Jesus began to speak of His approaching death, Peter, that impetuous spokesman of the twelve, took Him aside and began to rebuke Him. "No, Lord, this shall never happen to you." The idea that the King of Israel, the hope of the nations, the Savior of the world, should have to *die* was unthinkable to him.

But there is, perhaps, an even deeper reason for the offense of the cross. The death of Christ lays bare our hearts, reveals what we are. It underlines the depth of our need, the gravity of our sin. How dark and deadly the human problem must be if it takes this to deal with it! Shrinking from that conclusion, unwilling to face it, many insist that there must be some other way. "We can't be all that bad," is the protest. But the Bible offers no other answer. In a world like ours, a world of rampant hatred, violence, and death, there is no remedy, apparently, except in a cross, where God takes upon His own breaking heart the worst that evil can do. Christ must be given up to death, His body broken, His blood poured out. Then, strangely, in the mystery of God's love life, like a lily from a dark marsh, springs up out of that death.

But there is one more startling factor in this word of Jesus about life. Listen again. "Truly, truly, I say to you, unless you eat the flesh of the Son of man and drink his blood, you have no life in you." Life comes only from Jesus Christ, only from His death for the sins of the world, and only to those who eat His flesh and drink His blood. What on earth can that mean? The whole thing must have sounded abhorrent to His first hearers. The drinking of blood, any blood, was expressly forbidden in the Jewish law. How could this man, who professed to be Israel's Messiah, speak of such a thing? To understand what Jesus meant, we need to look at the whole drift of His teaching in this chapter. He seems to link a number of human responses with the receiving of God's life. In addition to eating and drinking, we read about "hearing" and "coming." Each of these physical actions is an outward sign of a significant total response to Christ — that of believing. "Truly, truly, I say to you," says Jesus, "he who believes has eternal life." Somehow "eating his flesh" and "drinking his blood" are vivid expressions of what it means to trust in Jesus Christ.

How is that so? Think of it this way. Eating and drinking are voluntary, personal acts. The hunger strikes of prisoners or martyrs for a cause are proof of that. No one can be forced to eat. You can keep a man alive by intravenous feeding for a time, but no power on earth can make him eat if he doesn't want to. He must so choose. Believing in Christ, also, calls for personal decision. Parents, ministers, teachers, friends cannot do it for us. It cannot be forced upon us. It is our own willing response to what we know of Christ.

But there is still another sense in which eating and drinking picture for us what it means to receive Christ. What we eat and drink becomes, in a very literal sense, part of us. We are what we eat. Portions of food are assimilated into the living tissue of our bodies. In this way, partaking of food points to the most profound reality of our faith. When we trust in Christ, accepting Him as Savior and Lord, He enters our lives by His Spirit and imparts to us His own life. Hear how Christ Himself puts it: "He who eats my flesh and drinks my blood abides in me, and I in him." Faith brings about a vital union between believers and their Lord. He abides in them and they in Him. God Himself takes up His abode in human hearts and there restores to them true life.

The Lord's Supper is a rich reminder and confirming seal of this new life in Christ. There the eating and drinking of faith are beautifully expressed. As we eat the bread and partake of the cup in faith, we are assured that His body was broken for us, that His blood was poured out on our behalf, and that His risen life is given to us as our nourishment and our strength.

Now, then, how does a person "come alive"? How do we stop merely existing and begin living? Christ says that there is a way. We start by realizing our need of Him, recognizing that He died for us, and welcoming Him by faith as Savior and Lord. Then we really begin to live. But there is more to come — life more abundant. All that vitalizes our relationships, quickens our zest for living, and makes us new, whole persons, roots in a growing faith, a deepening fellowship with the Lord of life. We come alive more and more as we get to know Him better.

Have you found the life He offers? Are you ready to receive Him now, the ever-living One? Many good things around us (like those my friend saw at that country estate) may enrich the quality of our daily living, but in themselves they can never impart life. They cannot make us "come alive." For that we need a life given for us, and a life-giver. We need Jesus Christ.

1. How would you define "real living"?

2. Jesus teaches that apart from Him we are spiritually dead. How does this condition of "death" become evident?

3. How can Christ's death bring us life?

4. In what ways do "eating" and "drinking" picture for us what it means to believe?

9. Thirsty, Satisfied, and Overflowing

On the last day of the feast, the great day, Jesus stood up and proclaimed, "If any one thirst, let him come to me and drink. He who believes in me, as the scripture has said, 'Out of his heart shall flow rivers of living water.'" Now this he said about the Spirit, which those who believed in him were to receive; for as yet the Spirit had not been given, because Jesus was not yet glorified.

(John 7:37-39)

IT WAS THE crowning day of the feast in Jerusalem and the colorful procession had already begun. Ranks of white-robed priests wound their way down from the temple courts to the pool of Siloam. As they marched they were chanting with deep voices Isaiah's ancient word: "With joy you will draw water from the wells of salvation" (Isa. 12:3). Once the priests had filled their pitchers at the pool they returned, panting and perspiring, up the steep ascent to the temple area. At the height of the celebration each would pour out his vessel of water before the Lord. It was Israel's way of recalling and celebrating how God had been with them in the wilderness, how He had fed them with manna from heaven and refreshed them with water from the smitten rock. Suddenly, in a hushed moment, a man stood

65

forth from the crowd and called for everyone's attention. "If any one thirst," He cried, "let him come to me and drink!"

It was a strange thing to say. What did He mean — "if any one thirst"? A thirst is a craving for something, a need that clamors to be satisfied, an emptiness longing to be filled. Maybe some of you know what it is like to go without water for a long time. You discover then that physical thirst is not a minor need, not a whim which you may or may not decide to satisfy. Rather, it comes as a life-and-death yearning, the cry of the body for what it must have to survive. We can go without food for days, even weeks; but we may die in a matter of hours for lack of water.

When Jesus startled the crowd on that day He was not offering them H_2O. He was speaking to an inner thirst. He seems to say that human hearts crave refreshment just as eagerly as parched throats and cracking lips cry out for water. In that sense He speaks to all of us. For what are we, we human creatures, but quivering bundles of need? What is our life — the struggle for fulfillment, the quest for happiness — but one long burning thirst?

The sad thing is that people often misread this thirst of the heart. They think it can be satisfied by the things around them. New Orleans each February celebrates Mardi Gras. A few years ago a number of us shared in an evangelistic ministry there called Mardi Gras Experiment. We were trying to communicate the message of Christ to the visitors, especially to the thousands of young people who come to the city for the festival. Mardi Gras has much that is bright and colorful but much also that is hollow and sad. To walk down Bourbon Street at the height of the festivities is quite an experience. Amid the surging crowds you see face after face that seems vacant and mindless. The thousands of empty wine bottles in the gutters speak their poignant message. Here are crowds of people trying to satisfy something inside them with cheap wine, drugs, burlesque shows. Someone has told them that New Orleans is "the city that care forgot" and that at the Mardi Gras you can be "king for a day." Here's where people are supposed to find what they're really looking for. But how many of them go away empty!

A thousand voices from the mass media besiege us with the same kind of message every day, trying to make us believe that fulfillment and satisfaction can be had in what they're selling. The promises are grand. But "what you can depend on" turns out to be a detergent, "the real thing" is a soft drink, and "something to believe in" is a new car.

And so the inner thirst, unsatisfied, keeps driving people on. Some think that a new home, a better job, or a different lover will quench it. For others it may be plunging headlong into one's work, or a busy round of parties and socials, bridge and golf. Maybe that can make us forget the gnawing deep inside.

Jesus Christ looked on all that — and looks on it still — with a breaking heart. "Why," in the words of the ancient prophet, "why do you spend your money for that which is not bread, and your labor for that which does not satisfy?" (Isa. 55:2). Why will you turn away from the fountain of living water to root around in barren gullies? Why push away the cup of life and try to store up refreshment in your own leaky containers? What could be sadder than that?

The thirst of the heart, whether men realize it or not, is a thirst for God. The psalmist knew it: "As a hart longs for living streams, so longs my soul for thee, O God. My soul longs for God, for the living God" (Ps. 42:1, 2). Augustine, that libertine turned saint, knew it too. "Thou hast made us for Thyself and our hearts are restless until they rest in Thee." Nothing else in the wide world can really fill the smallest human heart. There is a God-shaped space there, too big for anything else. Only He will do.

But listen to what Jesus dares to say: "If any one thirst, let him come to me and drink." There at the feast, where God's provision for His people was being celebrated, Jesus claimed to be the One who provides it! All that they remembered, hoped for, and needed, He was. "I'll do for you," He says, "what only God can do."

And somehow, when Jesus Christ talks like that, no one laughs. Words that would sound arrogant and preposterous from anyone else are believable when He speaks them. He does for people what only God can do.

When anyone really meets the living God, his life is satisfied, even though his immediate needs may not be met. Remember Job's experience? In a whirlwind of tragedy he loses family, possessions, and health. He cries out to God with anguished questions. He finds no answers from his friends and would-be comforters, but finally encounters God in a personal way. Job speaks: "I had heard of thee by the hearing of the ear, but now my eye sees thee; therefore I despise myself, and repent in dust and ashes" (Job 42:5, 6). His questions weren't answered, his problems weren't solved, but his heart was at rest. He had met his Lord.

What God did for Job, Paul found that the living Christ did for him. Paul had his thorn in the flesh — something embarrassing, painful, humiliating. Three times he prayed that it might be taken away, but the only answer he received from the risen Lord was this, "My grace is sufficient for you." And it was. "I will all the more gladly boast of my weaknesses," Paul exulted, "that the power of Christ may rest upon me" (2 Cor. 12:9). You know, too, of people hurled about and hurt by life, sufferers who battle against crushing odds, who yet find Jesus Christ sufficient for their need. Some of us have known the heartbreak of a child with affliction; others live with the never-ending ache of bereavement. Yet we find in the midst of our pain that Christ sustains us.

He satisfies, in a way we cannot fully describe, the thirst of the heart. He gives a sense of forgiveness, acceptance, and belonging to people who hunger for that. He gives security and hope to the anxious in the knowledge that their lives are in His hands. Our yearnings for meaning and purpose in life find their fulfillment in Him. And with it all He gives a personal fellowship, a transforming friendship, a love that warms and heals.

It's good to know this living Lord, Jesus Christ. I'm thrilled to speak about Him, not only as an escape from judgment, a Savior from death, but also as one who satisfies, as the One who is enough, sufficient for us all. A familiar hymn celebrates that: "I heard the voice of Jesus say, 'Behold, I freely give the living water; thirsty one, stoop down and drink, and live.' I came to Jesus and I drank of that life-giving stream; My thirst was quenched, my soul revived, and now I live in Him." That says it well. If you come to Him with all your heart, He will fill your cup. He will refresh you with the living water of His Spirit.

But the quenching of our thirst is not the end of it, either. Listen to His further word: "He who believes in me, as the scripture has said, Out of his heart shall flow rivers of living water." When you come to Christ with your thirst, surrendering to His lordship, something more will happen. Rivers of living water will begin to pour forth from your life.

What can that mean? Jesus appeals to this word as a promise of Scripture. Biblical scholars are not clear as to which Old Testament text Jesus had in mind. But there is one remarkable passage from the visions of Ezekiel which illumines this word. Ezekiel sees waters issuing forth from the temple, getting deeper and deeper as they flow, bringing life and refreshing to a desert wasteland all around. The temple of God has become

69

a source for life-giving streams. Now remember what Jesus said about the temple? He spoke of the temple of His body, the body which was to be pierced on a cross, and from which flowed blood and water. It is from Christ, in whom God dwells with us, that the living water flows. What is more, this crucified Lord is now risen, ascended, and has sent forth His Spirit to His people. Now it can be said that the Church of Jesus Christ — even the body of each believer — is a temple of the Holy Spirit. From Christians, themselves, the life-giving waters now overflow. As the Holy Spirit works through us, Christ's own life comes forth from within our inmost selves. Here is the secret of joyful witness and fruitful service. We go to Christ in thirst, commitment, and prayer. He fills us. And then, sometimes without our being aware of it, His life is communicated through us to others.

There is a Reformed church in Michigan where a dear friend of mine is the pastor. The people of the congregation have had great difficulty in trying to grow trees and shrubbery on the church property. Everything planted, however frequently watered, however richly fertilized, seems to wither and die. It's discouraging. If only some life-giving power could go forth from that church building to make the land around it blossom and produce! That doesn't seem to happen. But something more remarkable can happen and does. When Christians have found their own hearts satisfied in Jesus Christ and have experienced the fullness of His Spirit in their lives, a quickening power goes forth from them. Weary, careworn people are refreshed. Barren homes and hearts around them begin to blossom, and the spiritually dead begin to live again.

How is it with your life? Rivers of refreshing or barely a trickle? Has that inner thirst been really satisfied? Come with it all to Jesus Christ. Open your life fully and gladly to the fullness of His Spirit and then see what a difference the overflow can make!

QUESTIONS FOR DISCUSSION

1. What are the deepest, most basic needs of all human beings?

2. Which of these does Christ satisfy, and how?

3. How have you found Christ to be "sufficient" in meeting your needs?

4. According to Jesus, what must be true of our lives if they are to bring refreshment and new life to others?

10. The Road to Freedom

Jesus then said to the Jews who had believed in him, "If you continue in my word, you are truly my disciples, and you will know the truth, and the truth will make you free." They answered him, "We are descendants of Abraham, and have never been in bondage to any one. How is it that you say, 'You will be made free'?" Jesus answered them, "Truly, truly, I say to you, every one who commits sin is a slave to sin. The slave does not continue in the house for ever; the son continues for ever. So if the Son makes you free, you will be free indeed."

(John 8:31-36)

THERE IS SOMETHING in all of us that wants to be free. Liberty is every man's dream. Hear it in the popular music of our time: "People Everywhere Just Gotta Be Free," "Born Free," "I Need My Freedom." Or, in that especially poignant lyric, "I wish I could know how it feels to be free."

Some time ago the Russian novelist Anatoly Kuznetsov defected to Great Britain. Later, he wrote back to his countrymen, explaining his action. He wanted to continue in freedom the work to which he had devoted his life. Here he speaks a longing common to us all. Minority groups across our country have been singing, marching, demonstrating for years in the name of free-dom. Young people on a thousand campuses are reject-ing traditional mores and groping after new life styles in search of freedom. And what must freedom mean to those who were prisoners of war in southeast Asia?

Just what is this liberty that men hold so dear and for which they are willing to give and sacrifice so much? What does freedom mean? At the very least, it means that we don't want other people controlling our lives. We don't want to be squeezed into anyone's mold. We don't want others to impose their will on us or to keep us from being and doing what we feel to be right for us. In the popular language of our time, we want to be able to "do our own thing." We want to be free.

Take that novelist, Kuznetsov. He could write novels when he lived in Russia, but the problem was that they always had to be censored before they could be pub-lished. The authorities had to make sure his writing didn't contradict the party line. And Kuznetsov couldn't stand that; so he left his country and took a new name. He renounced all that he had formerly written, declaring that he would now write under the name of "A. Ana-tol." Only the books under that new name were to be considered his own, because only these would be written in freedom. He wanted to write what was in him to write. He wanted to be free.

And the blacks in our country don't want to be forced into a white man's mold. They don't want to be boxed in by a racist society. They want to be able to live in any neighborhood where they have the means to purchase a home. They want equal opportunity for every job that they have the qualifications to secure. They want the right to belong to any group which they have the credentials to join. They want to be free.

Many of the young people in our society feel the same way. They resist being conformed to a culture whose values they seriously question. They want to try their own way of life, live by their own values, be themselves, whatever their elders may think. They want to be free.

But what if a man gains all these freedoms? Suppose he lives in a nation with a high level of political liberty. And suppose he has found his place in the sun and has as many rights and privileges as anyone else. Suppose he has succeeded in breaking with many of society's petty norms. Does that mean he is really free? In the deepest sense — no. According to Jesus Christ, a man may have all these things and still be a slave.

That thoughts raises the hackles on many of us. When Jesus spoke to His contemporaries about freedom, they reacted angrily. "We are the chosen people, Jesus. We are Abraham's descendants. We were never any man's slaves. What do you mean — we need to be free?" Can't you hear many Americans making the same kind of objections today? "This is a free country, man. Nobody tells me what to do. Nobody pushes me around. Are you trying to tell me I'm not free?"

Jesus knew, however, that there are many kinds of bondage. It's not only a political system that can enslave you. It's not only a social structure that can box you in. There is something inside each of us that has power to enslave. That's what Jesus meant when He said, "Everyone who commits sin is a slave to sin."

Think about it for a minute. If freedom means doing what you deeply want to do, are most people really free? Even if we don't take orders from anyone, we still may feel trapped and miserable. Sometimes we can be enslaved by our own desires. Watch that happen, tragically, in the life of an alcoholic. He takes the first drink because he wants to. Maybe for him it's a gesture of freedom. But in time, if he's a certain sort of person, the "want" becomes stronger, more demanding. It gradually overwhelms his better judgment. Even though alcohol may threaten his health, his job, his family, still his desire for it drives him on — perhaps to complete ruin. Or here is a young person who experiments for the first time with drugs. Maybe it's to prove he's not "chicken," that he's grown up now, that he's really a free person. But what started out like a little excursion into freedom soon becomes a trap. Our national news magazines have pictured some of the somber results: young people contorted in grotesque positions, dead from overdoses or impure doses of some potent drug.

Yes, we can see all that readily, but that's perhaps not where most of us are. We may know little of the grosser forms of addiction. But that doesn't mean we are free. Take a little thing like a lie. We may lie to save ourselves trouble, to free ourselves from an embarrassing situation. But once the lie is out, how often we need to cover it with another and perhaps another! Before we know it, we are caught in a web of falsehood and can hardly find our way back to the truth.

Or what about the teenager who takes the first step down the road to sexual license? It seems like the "fun" thing. Isn't everyone talking about sexual freedom these days? Doesn't the Playboy philosophy tell us that's the way to live? But the one step leads to another and still another, until one day he finds himself on a road that goes nowhere. He feels disillusioned and soiled and caught.

To go our own way, to give free rein to our own wishes — that always looks like liberty at first, but it's pretty grim to wake up and realize we are not on the shining uplands of freedom but in some prison of our own making. Yet that's the way it is with us — all of us.

But to each who senses something like that in his life, Jesus Christ brings good news. He says, "If I make you free, you will be really free." That is, you'll be able to do what you most deeply want to do. How about *that*? Did you ever think about Christianity in that way? Maybe it has seemed to you that being a Christian means doing a lot of things you don't want to do because God or the preacher or society says you

75

ought to do them. But Jesus talks about *freedom;* and if freedom doesn't mean doing what you really want to do, it's hard to see what it does mean. Any man who is doing what deep in his heart he doesn't want to do is still a slave.

Well, how does Jesus make people free? Listen to what He said to some who had made a start at believing in Him: "If you continue in my word, you are truly my disciples, and you will know the truth, and the truth will make you free." He talks about "continuing" or "abiding" in His word. How do you get started in it in the first place? Why, when you hear the good news that God cares, that Jesus Christ gave Himself for us and offers us new life. When you hear Him calling you to trust Him and to follow Him — that's how it starts. When, as well as you know how, you turn your life over to Him in gratitude and trust — that's when you're on the way. But that's only a beginning. If you keep on, if you continue, if you "hang in there," as it were, then you are really a disciple.

"But," someone objects, "I thought you were talking about freedom. This discipleship bit doesn't sound very free. Wasn't Jesus talking about commandments and obedience and bearing your cross? I don't see much freedom in all that." But, strangely, Jesus Christ says that along that road we're going to know the truth that makes us free. That truth, to Him, is of a personal kind. He *is* the truth. As we listen to Him, trust Him, follow Him, we get to know Him better; and that's what makes us free.

Yes, free, because knowing Christ transforms people. Something happens inside of us when we meet Him. By His Spirit He begins to change things around. You know how most of us are inside — pretty torn up and divided. Over here is what we ought to do and then over there is what we really want to do. And often what we end up doing is a shaky in-between. But Christ does something about that divided self of ours. He changes our wants, reshapes our ambitions, transforms our values. More and more, what He wants for our lives is what we want. His vision for us becomes our goal, too. We begin to taste what it is to be whole people: free men and women. We find ourselves wanting to do what we ought to do; and here and there, we are able to do it. And that is freedom.

It doesn't happen overnight, of course. You don't get rid of all your hangups in one dramatic moment. But you do know that something real is happening and you're on the way.

Maybe that seems like a dream to you. It seems impossible that you could ever break loose from the thing that grips you. It must have seemed that way to the young gang leader who once heard about Christ on a radio broadcast, right when he was planning a full-scale gang war. Then and there, he committed himself to Christ. But how could he ever get out of that gang? It was worth a man's life even to try. But he faced them that night, told them what had happened in his life, urged them to make the same decison, then turned around and walked away. Oddly, no one made a move to stop him. Some of the gang leaders testified later that it was as though something held them back from harming him.

I like to see his experience as a kind of parable for us all, a map that shows our road to freedom. Let's say you are in his shoes. Let that gang stand for anything that has a grip on your life, that has you trapped, that's keeping you from being the person you ought to be. Whatever it is, in the name of Jesus Christ, you can face it. You can say no to it and walk away free.

So whoever you are, covet to be a free person. Don't let anyone or any system make a slave out of you. Be your own man or woman, the unique person you were meant to be. But remember, there are two roads along which you can seek your freedom. One is the way of self-indulgence. You can throw off all authority; you can follow your every whim and indulge all your desires. But ask the people who go that way if it really leads to freedom.

Another road, a better one, beckons. You can turn your life over to Jesus Christ; you can listen to Him; you can walk with Him; you can know His power in your life. And surprisingly, along that road of commitment, you can find out "how it feels to be free." Maybe you stand at the crossroads today. Oh, listen to the call of Jesus Christ and step out on the road to freedom!

QUESTIONS FOR DISCUSSION

1. How does the freedom Christ offers differ from popular American conceptions of freedom?

2. What is the difference between "freedom from" and "freedom for"?

3. Where do you recognize the reality of sin's bondage in your own life?

4. When Christ frees us from some enslaving evil, does that mean we will never be tempted by it again? Discuss.

11. How Can We Be Sure?

He answered, "The man called Jesus made clay and anointed my eyes and said to me, 'Go to Siloam and wash'; so I went and washed and received my sight." So for the second time they called the man who had been blind, and said to him, "Give God the praise; we know that this man is a sinner." He answered, "Whether he is a sinner, I do not know; one thing I know, that though I was blind, now I see."

(John 9:11, 24, 25)

How CAN WE be sure about our religious convictions? How can we know, for example, whether or not the Christian faith is true? Let me suggest two ways: by a firsthand experience of Christ's power and by a growing acquaintance with His person. Convinced Christians, assured believers, know what has happened in their lives and who is responsible for it.

Look at this blind man of whom we read just now. When we first meet him, his knowledge of Christ is zero. He has never heard of Him, nor met Him, nor had anything to do with Him. Put yourself in this man's place for a moment. You have never seen a sunrise, or a world turning green in spring, or the tenderness shining from a human face. Your darkness has never been pierced with the faintest gleam of light. You are blind. More than that, you are blind *from birth*. It was not an illness or an accident that snatched your sight away. You have *never* seen. You came into the world with sightless eyes. People see in you, therefore, not merely an unfortunate victim but the hint of some sinful secret, some dark curse. A fearful judgment from heaven, perhaps, has overtaken you. The followers of Jesus inquire about you in somber tones, "Rabbi, who sinned, this man or his parents, that he was born blind?" This confirms to you what you already knew all too well. Your life is worthless, hopeless, illstarred from the beginning. You feel at times that it would have been better for you if you had never been born.

But then you hear another voice — altogether different. "It was not that this man sinned, or his parents, but that the works of God might be made manifest in him." Here is something you have never heard before. Its music wakens something in you. Jesus has said that "this man is here for a purpose." That's a new thought. You may have felt that others were here for some reason, but not you. What good are people like you? In your day, in your society, all the blind can do is beg. But now you find that your life somehow has meaning — in fact, the highest meaning of all. The works of God are going to be revealed in you.

You are just beginning to savor that heady new hope when you sense that He is approaching you; He is touching your face. You shrink back at first, but His touch is gentle. You feel something cool and moist covering your eyes. Then you hear His voice again, "Go, wash in the pool of Siloam." There is authority in that voice and a gracious note that kindles confidence.

You grope your way toward the pool. It isn't far away; you've been there many times before. You wonder what it's all about. You're excited, yet hardly daring to believe that anything can happen. Now you're there. You kneel by the pool and splash its waters on your face. And then — light! For the first time in your life you can see! You kneel there for a while, completely overcome, drinking in the brightness all around you. And it's real; it doesn't go away. You're sure of it now; it's a new world. You get up and begin to walk. It's the same ground beneath your feet, the same sounds around you, but oh, how different everything is!

People begin to notice you. "Hey, isn't that the blind man that used to sit here and beg?" someone says. "Yeah, that's the man." But another answers, "No, it couldn't be; but he looks like him." Amused at this little controversy, you set things straight quickly. "I'm your man. I'm the beggar all right, but I'm not blind any more." "What happened?" they ask. "How did your eyes get opened?" You say, "It was the man called Jesus. He made clay and anointed my eyes and said to me, 'Go to Siloam and wash.' So I went and I washed and I got my sight."

A crowd has gathered by now and you realize that you're the center of a great deal of interest. Soon you are brought to the Pharisees, the religious leaders. They inquire about how this happened and you tell them the same story. Their reaction seems strange. They say, "This Jesus can't be from God. He doesn't keep the Sabbath.'" But many in the crowd cannot accept that charge. "How can a man who is a sinner do such signs?" they ask. Soon a full-scale controversy is raging, and you are right in the center of it. They want your opinion. "What do you say about Him since He has opened your eyes?" And you answer, "He must be a prophet; He must be a messenger from God."

But these authorities are still disturbed. They want to get to the bottom of this. So they call your parents. Now you see them for the first time. They seem frightened under the cross-examination. "Is this your son who you say was born blind? How then does he now see?" Your parents are happy, naturally, about what has happened, but they don't want any trouble. "We know that this is our son and that he was born blind; but how he now sees we do not know, nor do we know who opened his eyes. Ask him; he is of age; he will speak for himself." And so for the second time they question you. "Give God the praise," they say; "we know that this man is a sinner." "Come on, tell us the truth," they seem to say. "We know all about this man Jesus." By this time you are thoroughly annoyed at what's happening. Here a man has given you the priceless gift of sight and they are carping about technicalities! So you give your witness: "Whether he is a sinner, I do not know; one thing I know, that though I was blind, now I see."

There is the voice of authentic Christian certainty. We don't have all the answers. We don't pretend to. We cannot counter every charge leveled against Christ and His cause, but we know what has happened in our lives. We know the difference Christ has made and to that we bear witness.

The strength of such forthright, artless testimony came home to me early in my own life. I had been a Christian for only a few months and was home on vacation from college. I was a green freshman, not knowing a great deal about Christianity or about anything else, for that matter. I met an attractive girl in church on a Sunday morning and asked her for a date later in the week. She accepted and I arrived at her home at the appointed time to pick her up. As sometimes happens, she was still in the process of getting ready, so I had some time to spend in the living room with her father. He turned out to be a militant atheist. From the time I sat down he began to bombard me with arguments against the Christian faith. He was determined to prove that no intelligent person could possibly believe in Christ. I felt pretty helpless. I had precious little intellectual equipment with which to fight back. But I remember saying that although I couldn't answer his arguments, I knew that Christ had come into my life and had made a big difference to me. Since then I have learned a good deal more and I think I could present a reasonable defense of the Christian faith, but I don't know that I could improve on that first witness. "One thing I know, that though I was blind, now I see."

And that kind of transformation is happening every day. I heard from a young man just recently who told about how his life was changing. He had always had a terribly low self-image. He had trouble believing that he was worth anything or that anyone could care about him. What was negative and self-destructive in his outlook seems now to be breaking down and a new power is coming into his life. He is praying for the first time in years, "Thy will be done"; and through the persistent love of a young girl, he's beginning to sense a greater love and to feel differently about himself. He can't analyze it or explain it or defend it all, but he knows it's happening. When we have felt the touch of Christ on our lives we have something that no one can deny or take away.

But there is more to Christian certainty than an experience. It is one thing to know the change that has come about in our lives; it is another to know the person behind it. This blind man had been given his sight by Jesus, and with that new vision of the world there gradually dawned a vision of who his benefactor was. He described Him first as "the man called Jesus." When asked about who this man was, he ventured, "He is a prophet." When contending with the Pharisees he became even more convinced. "If this man were not from God," he said, "he could do nothing." That much he knew. This Jesus had to be from God.

Then, having been ostracized because of his courageous witness, he met Jesus — saw Him for the first time. In fact, Jesus sought him out and said, "Do you believe in the Son of man?" The man answered, "And

83

who is he, sir, that I may believe in him?' He wanted to know. He was ready to learn. He was open to what Christ had to say to him. Then came Jesus' word, "You have seen him, and it is he who speaks to you." The once-blind man said, "Lord, I believe"; and he fell down and worshiped Him.

Christ spoke to him personally. Christ revealed Himself to this man. He became to him not merely an unknown benefactor but a personal Lord. The man was sure then — sure not only of a changed life, but of a life-changing Master. He could witness not only to his salvation but also to his Savior.

It's along this road that certainty comes. When we listen to Christ's word, when we respond actively to His call, He becomes increasingly real to us. We learn to say, as the Apostle Paul did, "I know whom I have believed." It's not simply the effects of Christianity that I know, or the doctrines about the Savior, but Jesus Christ Himself. And when once He makes Himself known to me, no one can ever convince me that He isn't real and that He isn't Lord.

I wonder, do you have this kind of certainty today? Are you sure about the Lord and about what He's done for you? Are you sure about the past because it is covered by His forgiveness? Are you sure about the future because He's coming to receive you? Are you sure about the present because your life right now is in His hands? Are you sure about life's meaning? Sure about where you stand? Sure about your destiny? You can be.

But the blind man's experience teaches us this: before you can be sure, you need to realize that you don't know it all. Jesus says that those who know they are blind can receive true vision, but those who think they see everything miss the truth when it comes. In a sense we're all like that blind man — without hope, without purpose, without the knowledge we most need, until Jesus Christ comes our way. We can say we don't need

Him. We can shrink away from His touch. We can say that His word, "Go and wash," doesn't make any sense and won't do any good. We can remain as we are. But if we will listen to Him, if we will take a simple step in response to His word, we'll experience His power in our lives and we'll begin to know Him in a personal way. And then, thank God, we can be sure, convinced, unashamed.

QUESTIONS FOR DISCUSSION

1. How does assurance about our Christian faith differ from the kind of certainty we can have in, say, mathematics?

2. What is the relationship between direct personal witness and a reasoned defense of the Christian faith? In what circumstances would each be most effective?

3. Should every Christian be able to point to definite, observable changes which Christ has brought about in his life? What if he became a Christian while still very young?

4. What have you found most helpful in deepening your personal knowledge of Christ?

12. How to See the World

*I am the good shepherd; I know my own and my own
know me, as the Father knows me and I know the
Father; and I lay down my life for the sheep. And I
have other sheep, that are not of this fold; I must bring
them also, and they will heed my voice. So there shall
be one flock, one shepherd.*

(John 10:14-16)

IN OUR GENERATION, a few select persons have been
able to see the world in a radically new way. I'm
speaking of our astronauts. A number of these men
have made the incredible journey to the moon and
from that vantage point have been able to look back at
planet Earth. They have seen what no earthlings had
ever beheld before. They have seen our world as a
lovely blue and white ball, suspended in a sea of
blackness.

Many feel that this new vision of the earth is the
most significant event in our space exploration to date.
Through these astronauts, and the cameras they carried
with them, all of us have been given a new sense of the
beauty and preciousness of this planet. We realize as
never before that with all human beings we are fellow
travelers through the void on this remarkable bundle of
life. Man can never be the same again, some are say-

ing, because he has seen the earth from a new perspective. What a debt we owe to these brave explorers of space!

We owe the same kind of debt, in a different way, to artists. They, too, help us to see in this world what had before escaped our notice. The story is told of Joseph Turner, the great English painter, that once, while painting a sunset, he was sharply criticized by a lady observer. "I've never seen any colors like that in the sky," she objected. "No, my dear lady," Turner replied, "but don't you wish you could?" Artists communicate a vision which most of us have never had.

But perhaps our greatest need for new perspective is in looking not at this lovely planet, but at the people on it. How do we see *them,* the billions of human persons in the world today? To the dictator, perhaps, they are so many pawns to be moved about on the chessboard of his power. To the ambitious politician they count as voters to support his candidacy. To the advertiser they are potential consumers for his product. To the racist they seem (those "different" ones, at least) inferior, unpleasant, troublesome. To the nationalist those "others" may be enemies or allies, but they always seem less significant than his own countrymen. To help us see this world of people in a new way, from a different perspective, we need more than an astronaut or an artist. We need someone who sees a sinning, struggling, suffering mankind with steady realism, yet through eyes of love and with visions of hope. You know, and I know, who best fits that description. It is Jesus — Jesus Christ.

What did He see as He looked out over the world of men? Listen: "I have other sheep, that are not of this fold." Jesus has been speaking of those who trust and follow Him as His "sheep." In that homely way of speaking, a tremendous claim appears. For centuries men had thought of God, the Lord of heaven and earth, as the shepherd of His people — guiding, protecting, providing for and cherishing His flock. But here the man Jesus claims that role as His own! He is "the good shepherd." God's people are His sheep.

"Not a very flattering designation!" someone objects. "Sheep, indeed! What about man's powers, his intellect, his creativity, his titanic strength of will, his world-transforming technology?" Christ saw all those gifts and capabilities in men, but He saw them still as dependent on their Creator, vulnerable to danger, prone to stray.

But what the image of the sheep expressed most powerfully was their preciousness to the shepherd. The sheep are loved. They have a special relationship to the shepherd. He knows their names; each is prized for his uniqueness; each is called by his own name. The shepherd feels toward these sheep as no hireling, no professional could ever feel. They belong to him. No danger or misfortune would ever cause him to forsake them. So precious are they to him that the good shepherd is willing to give his life for the sheep.

Now in saying this, Christ speaks first of His followers, the little circle of those who believe in Him as God's Son and as the Savior of the world. But He looks beyond them to all the world of mankind, across all the centuries of time and says, "I have other sheep that are not of this fold." That was one of the most shocking things He could have said to the people around Him. To their minds, all of God's sheep were within one fold, the chosen nation. If you were in the fold, you were O.K. If you were a child of Abraham, either by birth or as a proselyte, you were more or less "in." Beyond that fold, there were thought to be no sheep — only wolves! Or at least outsiders, strangers, remote from the circle of God's care. But here is Christ's word, "I have other sheep." There are more, many more, whom He calls by name, whom He leads, for whom He gives His life.

The narrowing, exclusive attitude of Jesus' countrymen was not a problem peculiar to them. It is our human problem. How easy it is for every group to assume the same attitude, to imagine that those within our fold are the ones in whom heaven has particular interest! How many of us church people have cherished through most of our lives the impression that the real believers, the salt of the earth, are within our fold, and those outside are second-rate Christians at best, if they have any part in God's kingdom at all! How far from the vision of Jesus Christ when He said, "I have other sheep, that are not of this fold."

Christ looks on all the world's peoples as those among whom His sheep are to be found. The mark of His own is that they heed His voice. They hear His gentle call in the Gospel. They respond to that call; they obey it; they follow and are drawn into fellowship with Jesus Christ the good shepherd. And to Him there are such people everywhere. He can see His sheep where others see nothing of the kind. He can see the gold gleaming where others have never discovered it, the rough diamonds hidden beneath the surface. He can look on blasphemers and persecutors and see in them apostles; on drunkards and sensualists and see in them future witnesses to His truth. He can see them in jails and ghettos and taverns and alleys and can say, "There are My sheep." They have not heard His call yet, perhaps. They have not responded to it. But they are there; they are His; they are waiting to be won.

To see the world from Christ's perspective is to look at people that way. We see our great cities, not only as full of crowds, of pollution and heartbreak and crime, but also as the haunts of His sheep. Who knows but that some of those who are roaming in street gangs, who are behind prison bars, who are addicted to alcohol and drugs are among His sheep? To see the world through the eyes of Christ is to recognize that everywhere there are those whom He means to win, and none who are so far away that they cannot be brought back.

If we see the world in this way, we catch a glimpse also of our task. Jesus says, "I have other sheep, that are not of this fold: I must bring them also." Hear that imperative note: "I *must* bring them." Jesus lived all of His life under the pressure of a great "must," a great necessity: the will of God. Throughout His ministry you hear Him saying things like this, "I do as the Father has commanded me." "I do always those things that please the Father." "My food is to do the will of him who sent me, and to accomplish his work." And it was the Father's will that these people, these other sheep that were not of the fold, should be brought in. And so it was for this that Jesus lived and labored. It was for this that He gave His life. His tears, His agony, His rejection were all endured for this — to bring His sheep to the Father's fold.

What of us? Do we see our task from His perspective? What about the work of bringing others to faith in the good shepherd? For Christ this was not something optional, not one objective among many others of equal importance. For Him this was the thing He had to do. And oh, what it does for us to be gripped by that conviction! There are many things to discourage us from the earnest effort to bring others to Christ. Our selfishness whispers, "Why bother?" Our laziness cautions us to take it easy. The efforts we do make are often met with accusations of "intolerance" and "spiritual imperialism." And before these accusations we seem to wilt. Sometimes we meet with rejection. Sometimes our labors prove unavailing and we begin to wonder if it's worth it. We only steer a straight course through all hindrances when we are mastered by a simple conviction; namely, this is God's will and I must do it. Has that entered into the fiber of our lives? Have we seen our task through the eyes of Jesus Christ as something that we must at all costs fulfill?

But that doesn't say it all. For Christ it was more than a necessity, it was a joy. For Him there was never any difference between His duty and His delight. For Him this work of bringing in the sheep was not only a duty imposed on Him by His Father. It was the thing

He loved to do and longed to do more than anything else. And when we see our task through Christ's eyes, it seems not only an iron imperative but a golden privilege to be able to share in the work of bringing others to God's fold. He thought it worthwhile to spend His whole life doing this. He thought it worthwhile to come from heaven for this, to pour out His life's blood for this. Do you see that work as He saw it? We cannot imitate what Christ did in dying for the sins of the world, but we can begin to imitate the spirit in which He did it.

There is one more element in Christ's vision which we can share. We can see the assured results that will follow from our witness. Listen again, "I have other sheep, that are not of this fold; I must bring them also, and they will heed my voice. So there shall be one flock, one shepherd." How good to know that! Jesus Christ is sure of it. With majestic authority, He promises that when this word of the Gospel is brought to men they will hear it. They will believe it.

Let us be sure of that. Everywhere we go, among every people to whom we minister, there will be those who hear and believe. Some, perhaps, will put us off; some will remain hard and indifferent; some will scoff. But praise God, some will believe! And that makes it worth everything. No matter what the group, what the community, what the nation, some sheep are there whom Jesus Christ will bring to Himself. And our task is to go and find them, to go and bring them. Or better, to be the agents through whom *He* will find and bring His own.

There came a time in the life of the Apostle Paul when he became discouraged in his work at Corinth. The Lord stood by him one night and said, "Paul, don't be afraid, I have much people in this city." That must have encouraged Paul more than anything else he could have heard. "I have many of My own here, Paul. You don't know who they are now. They may be in idol temples, they may be wallowing in moral filth, but they

91

are Mine and I'm going to bring them and they will hear My voice." Why is that? Because of the sovereign power of God's Spirit and the magnetic attraction of the cross of Christ. It is that which draws men. It is not the ethics of Christianity, its moral code, its philosophy of life. These are rich and profound, but they do not constrain men. These never save them; they never grip men's hearts and bind them to Christ with cords of love stronger than death. No, what does that is the story of a suffering Redeemer. That's what masters the heart, grips the will, moves the life — when once we catch sight of His cross. It is the Good Shepherd giving His life for the sheep who brings wanderers home. And beyond all divisions and barriers, in spite of all difference and distance, He, the "one shepherd," makes them "one flock."

He calls you today, this dying, rising Shepherd-Lord. Will you hear His voice and follow Him? Will you let Him bring you to the Father's heart and home? Will you join the other sought ones, saved ones, from every tribe and tongue, every people and nation? And will you, for His sake, see the world of people in a new way? May it be so!

QUESTIONS FOR DISCUSSION

1. How do you feel about people of other countries and cultures? Do they seem as important to you as your own countrymen? Discuss.

2. What special encouragement does this passage bring to those who seek to evangelize others?

3. In what ways can a strong feeling of nationalism endanger the cause of the Gospel?

4. What brings about a sense of urgency in Christians to win others to Christ?

13. Good Grief!

Then Mary, when she came where Jesus was and saw him, fell at his feet, saying to him, "Lord, if you had been here, my brother would not have died." When Jesus saw her weeping, and the Jews who came with her also weeping, he was deeply moved in spirit and troubled; and he said, "Where have you laid him?" They said to him, "Lord, come and see." Jesus wept. So the Jews said, "See how he loved him!"

(John 11:32-36)

"Good grief!" We've all heard that expression—from Charlie Brown and his *Peanuts* friends, if from no one else. Did you ever wonder how it got started? Really, it's a rather odd thing to say, a strange combination of words. What is grief, anyway? We usually think of it in connection with bereavement, the shock and sorrow of losing someone dear to us. But we can go through grief over other losses, too. A divorce or separation is a grief experience. To lose one's sight, or to have a limb amputated, to have a dear friend turn against you, or to move away from old acquaintances — all of these mean that something precious and important for our lives has been taken away, and we grieve.

Well, if that's what grief is about, how can it possibly be good? This loss, this desolation, this aching loneliness — what can be good about that? People mock us cruelly when they insist that any such suffering could be good in itself. But perhaps it's possible to talk about good and bad ways of dealing with grief. Nothing takes the pain and heartbreak away, but there are some ways of handling it that are far better than others. Sometimes, for example, people try to *deny* their grief. They hold up bravely in the funeral home and at the graveside. They are pillars of strength, supporting the very people who come to comfort them. Actually, they may be refusing to accept what has happened. Perhaps they keep the loved one's room just as it was before, as though he had never left. They live increasingly in a world that cannot be real.

Others *delay* the expression of their grief. They too are strong in weathering the first shock of their loss. They seem to take it in stride and carry on as though nothing had happened. A friend once told me of a woman he knew who did just that. She took the death of her beloved husband with remarkable fortitude and calm. Friends viewed her composure with admiration, almost with awe. But about three months later that same woman went to pieces completely at the death of her cat. Her grief was delayed, bottled up, and finally burst forth explosively.

But grief need not be denied or delayed; it can be expressed in healing ways. And that's what I want to talk about with you today. Look with me at the shortest verse in the entire Bible: "Jesus wept."

Perhaps you recall the setting in which this took place. Lazarus, the brother of Mary and Martha, and a close personal friend of Jesus, had become very ill. When word of this reached Jesus, He reacted strangely. He remained for two days where He was, showing no inclination to make the trip to Lazarus' home in Bethany. Then, after that unaccountable delay, He started toward the house of His friend. He spoke of the illness in such a cryptic way that even His disciples were puzzled. When He finally arrived on the scene, Lazarus was dead — four days in the grave. Both sisters remonstrated gently with Him, "Lord, if you had been here my brother would not have died." When Jesus saw Mary and the others weeping, He was profoundly moved. "Where have you laid him?" He asked. "Lord, come and see," they said. And Jesus wept.

A great deal is conveyed in those brief words. They teach us much that we need to know. For one thing they assure us that *to express our grief in tears is right and good*. It seems that one of the hardest things to keep in focus, especially for Christians, is the real humanity of Jesus. We see His deity, His divine sonship as so central to the Christian faith that we often emphasize this at the expense of His genuine humanness. Check yourself on that. Can you think of Jesus as having dandruff? Or boils? Or blisters on His feet? If that sounds irreverent to you, it simply proves my point: it's hard to think of Him as one of us. And I suppose that when many people read that Jesus wept they imagine that His lip began to quiver and His eyes became moist. But there was more; He wept. Real salt tears.

That simple fact destroys a number of false ideas. Take, for example, the idea that it isn't manly to grieve. In our culture and in many others, young boys are taught the notion by the time they are old enough to learn anything that "Real men don't cry." Maybe that's one reason we strong men prove to be so weak. We have such tremendous strength and self-control that we end up having more ulcers and heart attacks than those frail females who give way to tears. But here was a man, *the* man, God's idea of a man, and He wept.

The second false notion is that to weep profusely in our grief is a sign of weak faith. What? Weak faith in Him whose whole life breathed trust, who leaned hard upon His Father every day? No, the ideal of Christianity is not stoicism, not an escape from feeling. Some may greet the worst of woes with a shrug of the shoulder, but that is not necessarily a good thing. Faith and apathy are not the same. Christianity was never meant to stifle emotion.

Then again, some people shy away from expressions of grief because they fear that grieving may lead to mental illness. Nothing could be further from the truth. In fact, precisely the opposite is true. A remarkably high percentage of those admitted to mental hospitals are suffering from problems directly related to grief — and their failure to recognize and express it adequately. Sometimes weeping, weeping freely, far from being dangerous, can be the best kind of mental health insurance. So forget those myths about tears. Jesus grieved. Jesus wept. Never let anyone tell you that it isn't manly, or healthy, or Christian to cry.

But there is another great comfort in these words. They assure us that *our Lord is moved by our grieving.* Now there are many things in this account and in God's dealings with us that we cannot understand. We read that Jesus loved Lazarus and yet He deliberately put off coming to him at an hour of need. We can sympathize with Martha and Mary when they express that very human feeling, "Lord, if you had been here, my brother would not have died." How often have we said or felt something like that! "If only the Lord had been here." "If only things had been a little different, this wouldn't have happened." "If only my son had been assigned to another battalion." "If only we had checked with the doctor earlier." "If only we had remembered to fasten the seat belts." In all of that we are saying, in effect, "God, You could have prevented this, You could have arranged the circumstances differently." And that is true. He could have intervened, could have forestalled many of the heartbreaks that have come to us; but He didn't.

Why not? That's the tough question. That's where our answers completely fail. We just don't know. And perhaps it's better to acknowledge that than to be forever second-guessing the God whose ways are not our ways. We can't figure Him out. We don't know. But we do know something else of overwhelming significance: He grieves with our grieving. As the writer to the Hebrews put it, "He can be touched with the feeling of our infirmities." While He was here among us He looked on people with all kinds of need and pain and had compassion on them. He felt with them. He somehow shared what they were going through. And He is still the same, yesterday, today, and forever. And you know, in hours of desolating grief that is what we most need — not a lot of answers, not plausible conjectures about why things happen, but the support of those who care, who feel with us.

This came home to me powerfully a few summers ago in a small group of chaplain interns of which I was a member. It was proving to be a difficult summer for my handicapped son, but in the group I always talked about him lightheartedly, with a brave smile. One day the leader of the group asked me if that's how I really felt about what was happening in my boy's life. Suddenly the smile faded and I began to cry, longer and harder than I ever had before. All the pain and disappointment of years seemed to come pouring out. Some time later the leader of the group suggested that I face an empty chair and imagine that God was sitting there and tell Him just how I felt about my son's affliction. I did that. Then he asked me to change chairs and to try to imagine what God would be saying to me. I still remember the words that came. "Bill, you're My child. I know you hurt, and I hurt, too. But that's not the end of it. There are brighter things ahead. So hang on." This is the God we know in Jesus Christ — not distant and remote from us, but very near, coming to us to share our sorrows and bear our sins. He is the God who cares.

And even in the midst of tears, *He gives us hope.* The same Lord who wept at a graveside is the one who raises the dead. There is a kind of false hope that some grieving people have. It is the hope of denial, of pretending, of make-believe. What Christ gives is nothing like that. No, He summoned this man Lazarus from the tomb! He reunited him with his loved ones. It didn't last then, of course. Lazarus later died again. Even Christ cannot raise us to eternal life until He first passes through death on our behalf. But He assures us that on the other side, He is the resurrection and the life.

So tears are right and good, but someday God is going to wipe them away forever. C. S. Lewis, the late English critic and theologian, was a man who knew first-hand what grief could be. Married late in life, he found an undreamed of happiness with his beloved, only to see her taken away a few years later by a lingering, painful illness. He wrote about it honestly and poignantly in a little book called *A Grief Observed*. Two thoughts come shining through it. One is that God is a terrible antagonist who can hurt us more than we dream. But together with that, always in the background, is this refrain of hope: "All will be well, and all will be well, and all manner of things will be well."

Jesus, the weeping sufferer, is now Christ the life-giving Lord. So grieve now, all you who suffer great loss, and don't be ashamed to express your grief. But remember in the midst of it that somehow the hot tears of God are on your pillow, too. The night may be very dark, but cling to the hope He brings. This anguish — even this — can be swallowed up in the joy of a resurrection morning, through Jesus Christ!

QUESTIONS FOR DISCUSSION

1. In your family and among your friends, how is grief usually expressed?

2. Why are Christian people sometimes hesitant to show any signs of deep grief?

3. When you have passed through times of sorrow, which persons have been most comforting to you? Why?

4. What aspect of the Christian Gospel is most precious to you in times of grief?

14. A Strange Way to Live

Truly, truly, I say to you, unless a grain of wheat falls into the earth and dies, it remains alone; but if it dies, it bears much fruit. He who loves his life loses it, and he who hates his life in this world will keep it for eternal life. If any one serves me, he must follow me; and where I am, there shall my servant be also; if any one serves me, the Father will honor him.

(John 12:24-26)

THE RUSSIAN AUTHOR Turgenev sometimes told admirers about his heroism at sea. It seems that once when fire enveloped a steamer, he, Turgenev, kept his head in the midst of danger, comforting distraught women and encouraging all hands. But someone else who observed the incident describes it quite differently. He says that the captain had to reprimand this large young man for pushing his way into a lifeboat ahead of women and children, moaning all the while, "I'm too young to die."

It is easy for us to sneer at his mock bravery, easy to feel contempt for such cowardice masquerading as courage. But isn't he much like us? We like to appear brave. We want others to see us as noble, generous and self-sacrificing; but when the pressure is on we find ourselves "looking out for number one." Self-preservation remains our first law.

It isn't every day, of course, that we are in a situation as dramatic as a fire at sea. We can fantasize, too, about how valiantly we might act because those crises don't come along very often. Our temptation to save ourselves first usually comes on more ordinary days, in more commonplace ways. There is, for example, the pressure to save ourselves from *blame*. You know how Adam did it in the garden: "It was that woman You gave me, God. She got me into trouble." And then there was the ludicrous defense offered by Moses' brother, Aaron. After he had fashioned a golden calf for the people to worship, Aaron came up with this pathetic excuse: "The people gave the gold to me and I threw it into the fire and out came this calf." That was it, Moses, the fire did it!

We may laugh, but how like us these men are! When confronted with our own wrong we try to shift responsibility, to save our own reputation, often by sacrificing someone else's. One partner in a marriage fracas disclaims all responsibility by dumping the blame on "him" or on "her." Or here is a parent who tries too hard to show that he can't be held accountable for his child's actions. Or here is a nation like America, brought face to face with tragic wrongs, but sometimes trying to get off the hook by blaming Communists or radicals or blacks.

Maybe we are most tempted to save ourselves from ridicule. Remember Peter — bold, blustering champion for the Lord? How could he deny Jesus three times? In part at least, it was this: to identify himself that night as one of Jesus' followers would have meant being taunted and laughed at. And that's hard to take. When truth is unpopular and when the right thing is not the "in" thing, how easy it is to hedge a bit or at least keep quiet! Sometimes we're ready to forget convictions, conscience, everything, to avoid being scorned. After all, no one wants to make a fool of himself!

100

I once heard a minister speak to college students at a religious emphasis week about vulnerability — about letting our feelings and our weaknesses show. He illustrated vividly, personally, what he meant. He talked about how fat he was, how he shrank with fear from ever getting on a scale, how he told jokes on himself to cover up his embarrassment, how he never let anyone know how he really felt. He knew, just as all of us know, that to open up about ourselves is risky. We might get hurt. People might snicker and take advantage of what we say. So most of us play it safe.

Perhaps the temptation comes to us along another line. In the little things of each day, we often aim to save ourselves from inconvenience, from trouble. Your wife wants to talk, but you're buried in the sports page or watching the ball game. Your husband feels amorous, but you're not in the mood. Your children hunger for attention, but you've had a hard day — you don't want to be bothered. Your friends drain your energies by sharing their frustrations and problems, so you pull back and cut them off. All of us are in this self-saving business. The choice doesn't seem dramatic or earth-shaking but we're making it all the same. We're "looking out for number one."

Now what amazes us, shames us, and makes us wistful is to see someone now and then living in another style. Someone actually does what Turgenev only pretended he did. An acquaintance bears a load of undeserved blame and makes no excuses. A friend stands up for you, even when he gets laughed at for his pains. Or a family member reaches out to you with a caring that costs, and you don't know quite how to take it. We can't figure that out. Those people are really going against the grain! They're marching to a different drum.

There is one life that seems to have affected the whole world in that way — the life of Jesus Christ. He was different. All along the way He seemed to be resisting the pressure to spare Himself. Think about His testings in the wilderness. What was at the heart of them? "If you are the Son of God," suggested the tempter, "command these stones to become bread." "After all," he seems to say, "a man has to live! How long are You going to wait for God to provide? How long has it been now — forty days? You can handle the situation on Your own. Save Yourself." Or again, "Here are all the kingdoms of the world! This is the dominion, the lordship which You are meant to have. All of it can be Yours so easily! No unpleasantness, no disgrace, no cross. Here's a smooth road to the throne. Save Yourself."

Jesus heard that siren song again in the clamor of the crowd for a sign. He heard it in their whispered plans to make Him a king. He even caught it in the saccharine words of a well-meaning friend. When He began to speak of His coming agony, rejection, and death, Peter took Him by the arm and chided Him, "God forbid, Lord; this will never happen to You." Peter was alarmed, almost indignant. "All this talk about suffering, that's not for us. Get those morbid thoughts out of Your mind." But with lightning in His eyes Jesus rebuked him. "Get behind me, Satan! You are a hindrance to me; for you are not on the side of God, but of men" (Matt. 16:23). In that well-meant, affectionate pleading He heard the tempter's call again, "Save Yourself."

But the final struggle came on Golgotha. The taunts seemed to come from everywhere. There were the rulers scoffing: "He saved others; let him save himself, if he is the Christ of God, his Chosen One" (Luke 23:35). Then the soldiers mocked Him, offering Him vinegar to drink: "If you are the King of the Jews, save yourself." And even from the cross beside Him came words loaded with venom and scorn: "Are you not the Christ? Save yourself and us." Yes, that was His great temptation. From the beginning of His ministry until its anguished end, the pressure was unrelenting: "Save yourself." But never once did He give in. He set His face like a flint to go to Jerusalem, to Gethsemane, to Golgotha. And He never stopped.

Why? we wonder. That's a strange way to live. What was behind it? Surely it wasn't that He hated life. No one ever lived it more fully than He. Was He then a victim, resigning Himself to a fate He couldn't avoid? That seems more plausible, but it hardly fits the facts. Again and again He had opportunity to take another road, but He *chose* this way. He chose not to save Himself. Why?

The scene pictured in our Scripture passage can help us. It is the day we call Palm Sunday. Amid cheering crowds, Jesus has entered Jerusalem. Admirers by the thousands meet Him with smiles, hosannas, and palm branches. The disapproving authorities are shaking their heads, "You see that you can do nothing; look, the world has gone after Him."

Yes, it is "the world" in a way; for the crowd contains many visitors. Jews from all over the empire have come to the feast and there are even some God-fearing Greeks among them. Some of these Gentiles spy Philip, the disciple, and come to him with a request: "Sir, we wish to see Jesus." Philip tells Andrew and together they bring this message to their master. What would you have thought when you heard it? "Master, it's not only the crowds from Galilee and Judea who are hailing You as king. We've just been talking to some Greeks and they want to follow You, too." What could all this mean? The response He's been seeking, perhaps. Maybe the beginnings, the first fruits, of a worldwide ministry. It seemed that His future was bright and His work just beginning.

But Jesus' reaction takes us by surprise. He didn't smile with pleasure or hurry to meet these new adherents. He did, however, see their coming as a sign. "The hour has come," He said, "for the Son of man to be glorified." The disciples had heard Him speak of His "hour" on a number of occasions, but always up until now it was, "My hour has not yet come." Now it had struck. Here was the moment He had been waiting for. Then came these words, "Truly, truly, I say to you, unless a grain of wheat falls into the earth and dies, it remains alone; but if it dies, it bears much fruit." There, in that brief parable, was His life's secret. Here is why He refused to save Himself. The seed that shrinks from burial in the ground will never bring a harvest. It may be valuable in itself, put to any number of good uses, but its power to bring forth new life depends upon a kind of dying. Jesus saw His life — and His death — in that way. Now that the world seemed ripe for what He had to give, it was time for Him to die; for only out of that dying could new life spring forth.

Christ was speaking about resurrection, of course, about victory over death. But more than that; He spoke of *fruit*. "I," He said, "when I am lifted up from the earth, will draw all men to myself"! By the magnetism of the cross He will draw people from all over the world to find forgiveness and new life in Him.

That was why He would not save Himself — because He wanted to save *us*. He chose to die so that people like us could really live. And by His power within us we can begin to live in that strange new way — no longer self-saving, but self-giving. That was His further word for us. "He who loves his life loses it, and he who hates his life in this world will keep it for eternal life." If we make it the main aim of life to preserve our own well-being, to secure our own happiness, we're in the process of losing the very thing we're after. But if, out of love for Christ and love for people, we're willing to risk ourselves, we somehow find life.

Oh, that we could see that! Why do we find it so hard? Why is the temptation the other way so strong? I guess we're afraid that if we give ourselves up to Christ and to others, we'll have nothing left. We haven't really listened to His promise that if we lose our lives, we will surely find them. Listen to His further word of assurance: "If any one serves me, he must follow me; and where I am, there shall my servant be

also; if any one serves me, the Father will honor him."
It may seem like a strange way to live, this way of
dying first, of risking, spending, and loving; but it turns
out to be the only life with a real future. And remember, it begins for you when you trust in the One who
died and rose again to make it possible — when you
can say with personal conviction, "He loved me and
gave himself for me."

QUESTIONS FOR DISCUSSION

1. How does our "instinct of self-preservation" relate
to our Christian commitment?

2. In what ways are you most tempted to "save
yourself" at the expense of others?

3. Is self-sacrifice always a good thing? Discuss.

4. What were the great motives behind our Lord's
refusal to save Himself?

15. What It Takes to Join the Church

Jesus, knowing that the Father had given all things into his hands, and that he had come from God and was going to God, rose from supper, laid aside his garments, and girded himself with a towel. Then he poured water into a basin, and began to wash the disciples' feet, and to wipe them with the towel with which he was girded. He came to Simon Peter; and Peter said to him, "Lord, do you wash my feet?" Jesus answered him, "What I am doing you do not know now, but afterward you will understand." Peter said to him, "You shall never wash my feet." Jesus answered him, "If I do not wash you, you have no part in me." Simon Peter said to him, "Lord, not my feet only but also my hands and my head!"

(John 13:3-9)

WHAT DOES IT take to join the church? You can get a lot of answers to that one. Some people say that you're born in the church. Your parents belonged to it, so naturally you're in it too. It's something you inherit from them — like brown eyes, or long legs, or a quick temper. Being a church member, then, means being born into the right family.

For others, joining the church means knowing the right answers. Church membership is like graduation after a long course. You learn what's in the Bible, you study the catechism, and when you feel as if you know the teachings of the church, you join it.

For still others, joining the church means swearing off your bad habits. Someone says, "I don't want to join the church quite yet; I'm having too much fun. One of these days I'll straighten up and change my ways and become a good church member." There it's not so much the right family or the right answers as living the right kind of life that puts you on the inside.

Now many of the people who feel that way are not too much interested in joining the church. And who can blame them? If that was all it amounted to, I'm sure I wouldn't be interested either. Actually, belonging to the church means a great deal more than any of the reasons just mentioned. It isn't heredity or orthodoxy or morality that makes the real difference. Don't get me wrong. I'm not saying that those things are unimportant. Of course they're important. The kind of home into which you are born has a profound effect on your religious life. Further, it's vital to know the doctrines of the church. Faith without knowledge is a pretty empty thing. And certainly any religion worthy of the name will have far-reaching effects on how you live. But being a part of the church — that's something else again. Something more.

What is the church, anyway? The significant thing about it is not its building or its organization or its ceremonies. The church is primarily a group of people — people who belong to God and who are related to Jesus Christ and to each other in a special way. That's what I want to talk about today. What is this new relationship to Jesus Christ which makes us belong to God's people?

As we try to answer that, look with me at a striking scene from the closing hours of our Lord's ministry. He was sharing a last meal with His disciples on the night before His crucifixion. There was noticeable tension within the group as they gathered. Luke's gospel tells us that the disciples had been quarreling about who would be the greatest, the most important in God's new kingdom. Some were claiming the place of honor for themselves. Others were feeling indignant at such presumption. Maybe that was why no one bothered about the foot washing.

The washing of feet was an important kind of courtesy in those days. People, for the most part, didn't wear shoes as we know them, but simply flat soles held on with thongs. It didn't take long, walking on dirt roads, for a person's feet to become dusty and uncomfortable. When you were a guest in someone's home, reclining at his table, with your legs stretched out behind you, a slave was usually assigned to pour cool water over your feet and wash them. It was the kind of thing we do today when we take a guest's coat or offer him a cup of coffee. When no servants were available, the disciples probably performed this little service for each other. But on this night, no one wanted to. "Why should I serve them?" each man thought. "They're no better than I am. I'm nobody's slave!"

It was the last night that Jesus was to be with them and this is how they felt! They were hardly ready to hear what He had to tell them. And there was much He had to share. His mind was weighted with the most tremendous concerns. He knew that His hour had come. The climax of His ministry had arrived. Death and departure from this world were very near. If ever a man had reason to be preoccupied with His own thoughts, Jesus truly did at a time like this. But, strangely, His heart was with His disciples. John puts it this way: "When Jesus knew that his hour had come to depart out of this world to the Father, having loved his own who were in the world, he loved them to the end." One was soon to betray Him; others would forsake Him and flee. All seemed at this moment disagreeable and unlovely. Yet He loved them totally, completely. With the full consciousness that He was the Son of God and the Lord of the world, He got up and began to wash the disciples' feet.

Imagine that you were there. Amid the hum of voices Jesus gets up and takes off His outer garment. What's this? You stop what you're saying and exchange nervous glances with the men around you. Now He's wrapping a towel around Him and pouring water in a basin. By now that splashing is the only sound in the room. You feel embarrassed and uncomfortable. What you balked at, what seemed beneath you, He is about to do. Quietly He moves about the circle, washing grimy feet, rubbing them gently with the towel. Now He's coming toward you. He smiles, but you drop your eyes. It's hard to look at Him, hard to let Him do this for you. You feel angry at yourself and ashamed. Still, it seems cool and refreshing, and you are moved that He would do that for you.

Now He's approaching Peter. As usual, Peter can't keep quiet. "Lord, are You going to wash my feet?" There — he blurted out the question that was in your mind, the one you couldn't speak. Jesus said, "What I am doing you don't know now, but afterward you'll understand." That didn't satisfy Peter. He seemed so uneasy and heartsick about the whole thing that he drew up his knees and almost shouted, "You'll never wash my feet." Then the answer came back that startled you and Peter and everyone else. "If I do not wash you, you have no part in me."

Dwell on that word for a moment. "If I do not wash you, you have no part in me." There is the key to what Jesus was really doing with that towel and basin. He was giving them an example. They were learning from Him that true greatness doesn't wait for attention but stoops to serve. He was showing them what a lowly and practical thing it is to love people. And they would never forget that lesson. But there was more to it even than that. The foot washing, eloquent and moving as it was, was a sign of something more that He was about to do for them. He was ministering now to a need of the moment; soon He would meet their deepest need. Now He served by washing their feet; later His death would serve to wash them through and through. And He wanted them to know that they could not belong to Him without that cleansing.

Most of us begin with an attitude toward Jesus that is quite naive. We admire Him; we are attracted to Him. He seems like a worthwhile person to follow. Moved by His example, challenged by His teaching, we decide that we'll throw in our lot with Him. We'll follow in His way and do as He taught. We'll be lowly servants as He was. We'll join His crusade against oppression and injustice. We'll lift our voices too, prophetlike, against the status quo. And all of that is noble and well intentioned. But there still is that troublesome matter about His death. Why does He have to talk about that all the time? We get Your message, Jesus. We see how You want us to live. But now that You've shown us, isn't that enough? Why this cross? Where does that fit into the picture? And He seems to answer, "Why? I'm doing it for *you*." But like Peter we want to say, "Jesus, we're ready to follow You. We'll do anything for You, but do You really have to do this for us? No, You need not die. Surely that's not necessary." But then His word comes back, "If I do not wash you, you have no part in me."

That's what Peter needed to learn, what each of us must know. There is no living bond of fellowship with Jesus Christ without His cross, without the cleansing which He brings. Think of Him as example, way-shower, prophet, master — He is all of these. But if He is not Savior to us, then we are not truly His.

We'd like to come to Christ on our terms, wouldn't we? Yes, let Him help us toward the good life. Let Him teach us what we need to know. Let Him make us well-rounded personalities or world-changing workers. We're ready for that. What we're not ready for is the humbling word that we need to be washed. But that is what it takes to join the church. We begin, not by learning answers or obeying rules or making promises, but by accepting His gift of cleansing with a trustful heart. Out of that faith grows the distinctively Christian attitude toward Jesus Christ: a blending of penitence and gratitude, a sense of immeasurable debt to the One who saves us by His poured-out life.

Jesus does for us what we cannot do for ourselves. He lays aside His glory and gives Himself to make us clean and make us whole. To refuse His cleansing is to cut ourselves off from Him. I'll never forget the chilling, cynical words of a poem I read soon after I became a Christian. The tone was arrogant; the words bitter. The closing line was, "I want no Jesus Christ to think he ever died for me." That's the tragic thing man is saying when he will not expose his life to the washing Christ offers.

But every heart with a spark of true faith in it feels quite differently. When Peter heard Jesus say, "If I don't wash you, you have no part in me," his reaction was immediate. "Lord, not my feet only but also my hands and my head." "If that's what it takes to belong to You, Lord," he said in effect, "go ahead. Wash me completely. I don't understand everything about it, but what I want is to be with You." Peter still pretended to know better than the Lord, but his eagerness warms our hearts. He didn't want anything to separate him from Christ. But Jesus replied, "He who has bathed does not need to wash, except for his feet." He seems to speak here of a first, thorough cleansing which all of us undergo when we put our trust in Christ and give our hearts to Him. That has happened for every believer and doesn't need to be repeated. But all of us, cleansed though we may be, become soiled along the way every day that we live. Our fellowship with Christ becomes clouded and we need His cleansing over and over again. As John Calvin once put it, "Christ always finds in us something to cleanse."

How is it with you today? Perhaps you have never known Christ's cleansing at all. You've never trusted

Him as the One who died to make you clean inside, to make you pure in God's sight. The first step for you is to acknowledge your need and welcome the gift He offers. "Lord Jesus, I long to be perfectly whole . . . wash me, and I shall be whiter than snow." And if you do trust Christ, learn to submit every day to the forgiveness that restores you and makes you clean.

When we know that gracious healing in our lives, when we are willing to live as debtors to His mercy, then we find the power to follow Him in lowly ministry. We begin to love as we have been loved. Yes, if He *does* wash us, we *do* belong to Him; and then we belong to each other, too. That is the wonder and the joy of joining the church.

QUESTIONS FOR DISCUSSION

1. In your experience, what meaning has usually been associated with the phrase "joining the church"?

2. In what sense is our Lord's washing the disciples' feet an "example" for us?

3. Once we have trusted in Jesus Christ for our salvation, why do we need subsequent cleansings?

4. What is the relationship between personal cleansing and our loving service to others?

16. The Cure for a Troubled Heart

Let not your hearts be troubled; believe in God, believe also in me. In my Father's house are many rooms; if it were not so, would I have told you that I go to prepare a place for you? And when I go and prepare a place for you, I will come again and will take you to myself, that where I am you may be also.

(John 14:1-3)

SOME OF YOU have known what it is to be deeply troubled. I'm speaking now not of the common worries that bring disquiet to everyone, but of a more profound kind of disturbance that shakes us to the foundations. You might call it radical anxiety. Our worries focus on various real or imagined dangers to our well-being, but anxiety arises when the very meaning of our existence is called into question. Something looms over us that threatens to have an overwhelming negative effect. It seems that our life will disintegrate and what has given it significance will be lost. Maybe for you it has been the death of the dearest person on earth. Maybe it is the collapse of an enterprise to which you had devoted the best energies of a lifetime. Or perhaps it seems that someone you trusted implicitly has let you down, has forsaken you, and you wonder if anything or anyone can be depended on anymore.

The hearts of Jesus' disciples were "troubled" like that. The word literally means "shocked" or "convulsed." They had bound themselves to Him in a kind of all-out commitment. For His sake they had left the old surroundings and securities behind. He had stirred them to the depths and awakened unheard-of hopes in their hearts. Allegiance to Him had made them new persons and had brought a thrilling sense of purpose to their lives. Imagine what it was for them to be told that He, their leader and friend, was about to leave them! More than that, they learned that in the mysterious crisis ahead their own loyalty would collapse and they would be scattered from Him. No more desolating prospect could be imagined: to lose Him, the light of their lives, and to be lost themselves in the process.

Jesus must have seen the pain and despair in their faces "Let not your hearts be troubled," He said. Good advice, but often very hard to follow. People sometimes mock us with their well-meant exhortations. When we're depressed they urge us to cheer up; when we're scared out of our wits they tell us not to be afraid; when we're so tense we can hardly stand it they caution us to take it easy. Such advice in many cases is worth nothing at all. Our friends tell us not to feel so bad, but they give us no real help in feeling better. But Jesus had something more to give His disciples than general advice. Along with the invitation, "Let not your hearts be troubled," He offered them another way, a healing alternative. "Believe in God, believe also in me." As an antidote for the trouble in their hearts He offers them *trust*. "Trust in God," He says, "and trust in me."

The call to rely on God, of course, was not a new one. The God of Abraham, Isaac, and Jacob had been for ages the refuge and strength of His people. They were summoned again and again in the Old Testament to look toward Him in their distress. "Trust in the Lord Jehovah, for in the Lord is everlasting strength" (Isa. 26:4). "O house of Israel, trust in the

Lord, for he is your help and your shield" (Ps. 115:9). And with that call to faith came this word of assurance, "Thou wilt keep him in perfect peace whose mind is stayed on thee" (Isa. 26:3, KJV).

The new thing, the startling thing in the word of Jesus is the way He joins together faith in Himself with faith in God. The wording of the sentence in the original Greek brings the two together in the closest possible connection. He says, literally, "Trust in God, also *in me* trust." Jesus doesn't mean, of course, that there are two objects of supreme trust. He doesn't present Himself as a second security, an alternate refuge. He is saying that the ultimate trust we owe to God is rightly placed in *Him.* Jesus Christ is the full disclosure of God, the One in whom God comes to us, visibly and personally. Now that He has come, all genuine trust in the living God is inseparable from trust in Him.

Jesus was saying that sort of thing all through His ministry. He taught repeatedly that to see Him was to see the Father. To hear Him was to hear the Father's word. To receive Him was to welcome the Father also. And, since this was true, all men should honor Him even as they honor the Father. Now, in this passage, He urges His disciples to trust Him with the trust that only God Himself can claim.

Well, what does it mean to trust in Jesus in this way? And how can that give help to people who are deeply troubled? For one thing, it means to *believe His Word about the future.* This is one of the indicators of where our trust lies, isn't it? Whose word do we rely on concerning what's ahead? Jeane Dixon made a prophecy in 1968 that the Nixon administration would become involved in a wire-tapping scandal. Some are skeptical about such prophecies by Miss Dixon because many of her prophecies have not come true. People who do believe in Miss Dixon's prophecies, however, are directing toward her a remarkable kind of trust. When we believe and act upon someone's word about the future, we are in effect putting our future in his hands.

It is precisely that which Jesus Christ calls people to do. "In my Father's house," He says, "are many rooms. If it were not so, would I have told you that I go to prepare a place for you?" "You can trust Me about the future." He seems to say, "Would I have told you about these things if they were not true?" Jesus always spoke about the life to come with that calm sense of familiarity. He was like a mountain climber who has reached the summit long before the other members of his party and who reports back to them clearly and matter-of-factly what he sees.

What does Jesus say about the life to come, about the future that is ahead for His followers? He describes it simply and beautifully as "My Father's house." We've already met that language earlier in John's gospel when Jesus drove the money-changers out of the temple. Then He spoke with blazing eyes to the merchants around Him: "Take these things away; you shall not make my Father's house a house of trade." The temple, because it was the special place of God's presence on earth, could be called His Father's house. And He lets us know that the most heartwarming thing about our hope for the future is that we will be with God — in His presence.

But the "Father's house" expresses more than that. It conjures up all the memories of home. Not all of us, sadly, have been privileged to live in homes where love reigns and happiness dwells. For some, the memories and associations of family life are grim and painful. But where a house is a home, graced by a father's strength and a mother's tenderness, where ties are close and love runs deep, there we begin to sense the atmosphere of heaven, the Father's house. At least, it was that way for me. At home I always felt at ease, secure, believed in, and cared about. Home was a hearth to warm yourself by, a haven from storms, a secret place to gather strength. And in God's future for His people, all that is foreshadowed in the best of homes finds real fulfillment.

There are many rooms, many mansions, many dwellings, in the Father's house. Paul Tournier, in his book *A Place for You,* writes of the deep human need for a place to be. Our lives are never lived in the abstract. They are always localized. All experiences and feelings are joined in our memories with certain places. To exist for us is to occupy a particular living space to which we have a right. Watch the sea gulls perched on a railing. Ornithologists tell us that they always stand at least twelve inches apart. If another gull flies down between them they quickly fly away. All seem to respect the law that each has a right to his own living space. We are that way, too. Think what it means to have your own room, or even a corner that is especially yours! Each needs a place, a space that is recognized and respected by others. Christ's promise about heaven is that God has a place for us — our own place, where we belong, where we find room. When pilgrimage is ended, wanderings over, there's *home.*

Christ's other word about the future is that He is coming back to earth. "I am coming again." The Bible speaks of many comings of God to His world and to His people. He comes at times in the breath of His Spirit to renew His church. He comes also in terrible visitations of judgment. He comes at the moment of death to receive each of His people to Himself. But all of these are only hints in time of a final coming, a triumphant appearing at the end of the age. Why do we believe that, if we do? In part because we read the signs of the times, or because angelic messengers once assured His followers that it was so. But the Christian conviction at heart is based on His own word of promise: "I am coming again." To believe in Him is to trust that word — that promise of all promises — that Christ is coming back.

But a person can believe the word of Jesus about the future with unquestioning confidence and still fall short of full-orbed faith. Belief in Jesus is more than confidence in His veracity, more than reliance on Him as a true prophet. It has a dimension of *personal trust*. It appeals not only to His Word but also to His heart. To believe in God through Christ is to be persuaded that He is *for us*. It is to know that He has us in His heart, that He cares about us and seeks our good. And that is what dispels anxiety and scatters fear.

That's what the disciples needed most. That's what put Jesus' going away from them in a completely different light. Jesus said, "I'm going away"; yes, but He added, "to prepare a place for you." Only by seeming to leave them, could He provide for them all that He longed to give. Christ must give His life for them so that a way may be opened for them to live in God's presence. He must leave this earth and go to the Father so that one day there may be room in the Father's house for them.

His coming again is also linked to their good. "And when I go and prepare a place for you," He says, "I will come again and will take you to myself, that where I am you may be also." He goes away for them; He comes again for them. Love for His own is behind all He does and always will be. "Believe in Me," says Christ, "with that kind of trust. You cannot understand everything now. At times it will seem that you are being forsaken, left alone. Sometimes life will seem to cave in around you. Joy and meaning will take wings and fly away. Your hopes will sometimes be disappointed and you yourselves will know the bitterness of failure. But keep trusting in Me. Trust Me as the God who is more than enough for your needs, who has tomorrow in His hands, whose love will never forget you. Don't give up on this world. I am its Lord and I am coming back. And at the end of everything for you, there is room in the Father's house and a place at My side."

There, in any age and for anyone, is the cure for a troubled heart. Have you found it? Why not trust now in the God who comes to you in Christ? Believe His Word about the future, and count on it that nothing

118

will ever shut you out from His love. May His peace be yours!

QUESTIONS FOR DISCUSSION

1. What have been the most anxious moments of your life?

2. How would you explain the meaning of *trust* to a little child?

3. What has Christ clearly promised about the future? What things remain uncertain?

4. How do these verses help us in our understanding of the life to come?

17. One Way!

"And you know the way where I am going." Thomas said to him, "Lord, we do not know where you are going; how can we know the way?" Jesus said to him, "I am the way, and the truth, and the life; no one comes to the Father, but by me."

(John 14:4-6)

PERHAPS YOU'VE SEEN that familiar sign in a gathering of young people: a forest of raised arms, all with index fingers pointing heavenward. Many know it as a popular signal in the counterculture of our time. The message it proclaims is simple: "One way!"

That rallying cry, however expressed, is not peculiar to the so-called Jesus people. It springs from the very heart of biblical faith. In every age, in every place, Christians of all types have confessed in their witness before the world that there is "one way." If any Bible text has especially inspired that slogan, it is probably the one which we read today. These are the words of Jesus to His disciple Thomas: "I am the way, and the truth, and the life; no one comes to the Father, but by me." Here, briefly, in His own words, we have *Jesus' conviction about the goal of life, His counsel about how to reach it, and His claim to be the only way.*

First, He speaks of mankind's true goal. What are we really headed for, anyway? How are we to understand the final meaning of human life? Some would answer that question in terms of what we experience here and now. Life to them consists of the sheer fact of existence, of awareness. What happens to us, what we pass through during our days on earth — that's what life means, nothing less and nothing more. Presumably, then, the person with the widest variety of experiences — who most keeps in touch with things by press, radio, or TV — is living the most meaningful life. Live as fully as possible now; grab all the gusto you can. That, say some, is the goal of life. But curiously, many who have sampled everything seem to give way to despair.

Others see our true fulfillment as found in success or happiness. Regular increases in what we call "the standard of living" represent progress toward the goal. The swelling of our Gross National Product is the sure sign that we are on the right track. But if an endless succession of experiences fails to make life meaningful, the constant gathering of goods and honors does no better. There is a remarkable passage in Tolstoy's *Confessions* in which he describes how, as a man in his forties, successful, wealthy, happily married, with a large family and all the rest, he found himself hiding the rope which hung in his study for fear that he might take it and hang himself.

There are still others who would scorn selfish pursuits and insist that the goal of life is to create a perfect human society. Some would argue that the goal is almost within reach of our technology. By astute behavior modification, by genetic engineering, and unlimited organ transplants we can perfect human life on this planet — perhaps even eliminating death itself. This is the goal to give oneself to, we are told, or perhaps to a revolutionary social or political cause that is sweeping the earth. Strange, isn't it, how none of us would be prepared to argue that we personally are perfectible, and still dream that all of human society can be made into a paradise. We forget what happens even to the best causes and the best people when they finally come to power.

For Christ, the meaning of our existence is to be sought elsewhere. For Him, the true direction of life is Godward. It lies in our relationship to the maker of heaven and earth. Jesus said of Himself that He was going to the Father and that the destiny of His followers was to be with the Father also.

In other words, the meaning and goal of life cannot be found within ourselves. When we search for it there, we seem to wind up either living on a merely animal level or vainly imagining that we are gods. We can only rightly know ourselves and what we are meant for when we know the One who made us. We were created for Him and for each other. Fellowship with Him as His people is our true destiny. No perspective on life which leaves God out can finally satisfy the human spirit. The famous word of Augustine still stands and is freshly verified every day: "Thou hast made us for Thyself, and our hearts are restless until they rest in Thee."

What about you? What would you say that your goal in life is? Get an education, get a job, get married, raise a family? All that is fine. Develop your abilities, do something creative, make a contribution to society? Worthy aims, all of them. But think beyond them for a moment. Is there any ultimate purpose that binds all of that together? Are you here to know God, to worship Him, to serve and enjoy Him forever? Jesus said that's what it's all about. Without that we've missed it, whatever else we may do.

Well, if that is the goal, how do we get there? That was Thomas's problem. He was confused, almost exasperated, when Jesus began to speak about these things. He broke in abruptly, "Lord, we do not know where you are going; how can we know the way?" Jesus' answer was short and to the point: "I am the way."

It isn't easy to take in the magnitude of that confession. Jesus has been telling His disciples that human life finds its deepest meaning in relationship to our Maker. Our highest destiny is to be loved by God and to love in response, to obey Him in trusting commitment, and to live with all His children in God's "forever family." Now Jesus calmly teaches that He Himself is the road to that goal.

When Jesus goes on to say, "I am the truth," He is showing more fully how He is the way. To dwell forever with the Father means *knowing* Him, and Jesus Christ is the true revelation of the Father. In Him the truth of God becomes visible. In Him the living God makes Himself personally known. God can be known only as He pleases to draw back the veil and reveal Himself. Our senses cannot perceive Him, our minds cannot reach up to grasp Him. We can never know what He is really like until He opens His heart — until He lets us know the truth. Christ is the way because in Him we come to know the Father. In the life and ministry of Jesus and supremely in His death and Easter victory, God shows us who He is and how He feels toward us. Jesus can say, "He who has seen me has seen the Father." That's why He is the way.

Take that other great word, "I am the life." Again, this further develops how Jesus is the way to God, to fellowship with God, and likeness to Him. If we are to enter God's kingdom, says Jesus, we must be "born again." Flesh and blood, human nature as it is, cannot inherit the heavenly kingdom. In our wandering from God, our ingratitude, our rebellion, we have lost our true life. Physically alive and mentally alert, we remain spiritually dead. We need a new birth, a new beginning. We need new life, God's own life, a life that even death cannot destroy. And Christ claims that that life is in Him. He has come that men and women may have it. In Him we find not only the knowledge of the true God but also the power to be transformed into His likeness. In Christ we learn that God is a gracious Father to us, and in Him we receive the power to

123

become His children. He both reveals God to us and makes us fit to live in His presence. That's why He is the way.

And think of it, these words were spoken shortly before Jesus gave Himself up to be crucified. What a tremendous affirmation of faith! He said He was the way, but when He died it seemed that there was no way at all. He claimed to be the truth, yet it seemed that lies had conquered and destroyed Him. And how could He be the life if death had claimed Him after all?

But it was by that very cross that Christ became the way, the door into the Father's house, the one mediator between God and men. There the truth of God came fully to light — His holy wrath against sin and His sin-bearing love for us. And by descending into death and taking its worst on our behalf, He became the Prince of life. Now He ever lives to be the way, the living way.

And Christ leaves no doubt about the full extent of His claim. He not only says, "I am the way," but He makes it perfectly plain that He is the only way. "No one comes to the Father," He says, "but by me." Here is where many take issue with Him. There have always been people who think highly of Jesus, who respect His character and cherish His teachings and yet reject His exclusive claim. The religions of the East, for example, are broad and inclusive. They have a place for Jesus. They assign Him a high rank, together with other great religious teachers, other agents of revelation, other manifestations of the divine. But they do not yield to Him a solitary throne.

Christian missionaries are sometimes strongly criticized for their insistence that Christ is the one way to the Father. That strikes people sometimes as another brand of imperialism. Here are proud Westerners saying that their religion is better than anyone else's! To present Jesus as the only way is said to be narrow-minded and intolerant. The religion of the future, some contend, is to glean the best of all the world faiths.

Since we're all headed in the same direction, why not accept each other's truth and walk together?

Is it sheer stubbornness, then, when Christians continue to confess "one way"? Certainly none of us are free from the pride of opinion that insists on being right. But there is more involved than that. Christians hold that Jesus is the one road to the Father's house precisely because that is what He claimed. We make that confession out of loyalty to Him. We see in all the great religions of the world much of noble striving and keen insight, much earnest searching for the truth. But we confess that in Jesus Christ God has done something completely unique. He has come to this earth in the person of His Son to bring us into a new and right relationship with Him. Christ is God's voice calling to us, God's heart yearning over us, God's hand reaching down to us. To ignore that loving, divine approach, to refuse that way and insist on finding one of our own, is to miss life's meaning and to abandon hope of reaching its goal. Humanly speaking, we would like to believe that all the roads on which men are walking eventually lead to God, but Christ lovingly warns us that it is not so.

Suppose for a moment that you were lost in the heart of the jungle. Near at hand are tigers on the prowl, poisonous snakes, and many other unknown perils. You don't know which way to turn. Without help, you're certain to perish. Suddenly a man appears who promises to be your guide. He says to you, "Follow me; stay right behind me; walk where I walk; stop when I stop. Do exactly as I tell you and I'll lead you to safety."

Now everything depends on whether or not that man is trustworthy. He may be leading you to death or into the hands of enemies. If you believe that, you will probably ignore him and stay where you are. But suppose he's telling the truth. Suppose you believe him. Then you will concentrate all your energies on following him.

Not all the guides that offer us a way to heaven and home are trustworthy. But consider Jesus Christ. One who loved you enough to die for you is not likely to lead you astray. He is worth trusting. And it is Jesus the faithful witness, not some overzealous follower of His, who says, "I am the way . . . no one comes to the Father, but by me."

But don't stop at hearing that. If He's the guide, follow Him. If He's the way, walk in Him. If He's the truth, believe Him. If He's the life, live Him. Put your whole trust in Jesus Christ and as you do, you have His word: that way leads to the Father's heart and to the Father's house.

QUESTIONS FOR DISCUSSION

1. What happens to us when we search for life's meaning and goal simply within ourselves?

2. How would you formulate your most significant goal in life?

3. How would you answer the charge that Christ's claim to be the "one way" is "intolerant"?

4. What is the difference between preaching the "offense of the cross" (Christ's exclusive claim) and preaching the Cross offensively?

18. Where to Look

*Philip said to him, "Lord, show us the Father, and we
shall be satisfied." Jesus said to him, "Have I been
with you so long, and yet you do not know me, Philip?
He who has seen me has seen the Father; how can you
say, 'Show us the Father'? Do you not believe that I
am in the Father and the Father in me? The words that
I say to you I do not speak on my own authority; but
the Father who dwells in me does his works. Believe
me that I am in the Father and the Father in me; or else
believe me for the sake of the works themselves."*

(John 14:8-11)

"LORD, SHOW US the Father and we shall be satisfied."
That's a different view of satisfaction, isn't it? One
would think from a few samples of modern advertising
that satisfaction is readily available anywhere. How
many products that you have heard about guarantee
"satisfaction or your money back"? I can remember a
cigarette ad (which has now gone the way of all slo-
gans) which used to make that total claim for its brand
of smokes: "They satisfy." The implicit promise is
always this: If you buy and use what we are offering,
you'll be happy with it; it will meet your needs; it will
fulfill your desires; it will make your life complete.

And there's no doubt that many of our needs *are*

satisfied in the abundance which our technology spawns. When we're thirsty there are beverages to quench that thirst, and all kinds of foods to still the cry of hunger. There are pills to ease our pains, sprays to keep us dry and fragrant, mouth washes to make us appealing. Whatever need or problem a person has, there is always someone promising to take care of it.

Perhaps that's the saddest of the deceptions with which we live in our society — the idea that goods and gadgets can be secured that will satisfy us all. We seem to keep on believing it even when those who buy almost everything remain restless and empty.

Happily, there are voices being raised in our culture that expose this big lie. Hosts of young people refuse to believe it. More of us are realizing that with all our affluence, many of our needs go unmet. How can a person be satisfied, no matter what he has, if he has never learned to love or be loved? How can we be genuinely fulfilled without some encouragement from other people? As Victor Hugo put it, "Man needs affirmation more than he needs bread." Without a wholesome self-respect, without some sense of purpose for our lives, nothing quiets the rumblings of discontent deep down inside us.

But suppose now that you're in fairly good psychological health. You have warm, wholesome relationships with the people close to you. You feel pretty good about yourself. You have a job to which there is at least some purpose. There are friends around you who give your ego a much-needed boost now and then. With all that, it would seem that you have it made. But does it always work that way?

I guess it depends on what we think human beings are. If we are only animals, then the fulfilling of our animal wants ought to be enough. If we are sophisticated social animals, then the enlightened supports of society should take care of all other needs. But if we are more than all that, if we have something of eternity in our hearts, an insatiable quest for meaning, if we

128

were made for something more and greater than our immediate environment, then no matter what we have or who is around us, we will still be searching for something. And many of us seem to be on that kind of search. Philip expresses this deeper human need: "Lord, show us the Father and we shall be satisfied." To know God, the source of all that is, the mysterious meaning and power behind the universe — that, to Philip and many others, is what we finally need to satisfy us.

It isn't that we know nothing at all about the Creator. This earth so filled with marvels and the vast reaches of space beyond us speak volumes about Him. What colossal power, what amazing ingenuity, must have brought all this into being! What evidences of order, what breath-taking works of beauty we see all around us! Sunshine and rain, a prodigally fruitful earth, the returning of life in the spring — all this must say something about a cosmic benefactor who cares for this earth.

But many moderns, surrounded by all this and knowing more about it than anyone ever has before, still find in the creation no satisfying knowledge of God. What we call "nature" seems to speak a double message. There is order and provision, yes; but there is also chaos and death. This fair earth has its floods and earthquakes, its famines and plagues. The same nature that appears friendly to mankind in general can seem at times to crush individual human lives with mindless or even cruel force. If God is to be known through the disasters and evils that often visit this planet, then that knowledge is hardly reassuring.

What do we really need to know of God to have our hearts at rest? At least this: how He feels about us, how we stand with Him. And that, even the creation with all its eloquence cannot disclose. As a great theologian once put it, "In the world around us we see God's hands and feet but not his heart." And precisely that — His heart — is what we need to know. To be shown who He is and how He feels toward us, to come to clarity and certainty about God and to see all of life in the light of that knowledge — that can satisfy us. And this man Philip seemed to believe that Jesus Christ could provide that. Hence, is plea: "Lord, show us the Father, and we shall be satisfied."

Here is the heart of Jesus' answer: "He who has seen me has seen the Father." To the request, "Show us the Father," Jesus responds, "Philip, that's what I've been doing all the time I've been with you. I've been showing you the Father." Philip, perhaps, was looking for something spectacular. He remembered in his Old Testament heritage how God had revealed Himself once on a blazing mountain amidst thunder and lightning, clouds and thick darkness, with what sounded like the blast of trumpets. He longed for some visible demonstration of God that would overwhelm all doubts. We are like him in that. We hunger for the extraordinary, the sensational. We crave some immediate awareness of God, some flood tide of religious experience, perhaps, that will inspire us all our days. But Jesus says that the vision of God which we most deeply need is given openly in Him. That is the truly staggering word of the Christian faith: not simply that Jesus is like God, but that *God is like Jesus.* When we have really seen Christ, we have seen God. That is, we know God best when we behold Him in that one remarkable life.

How does God feel about the sick and afflicted of the world? Watch Jesus as He touches, comforts, and heals them. That's how. How does God look on the cruelty that oppresses little people and the pride that scorns them? Look into the blazing eyes of Jesus as He defends such people and you will see. What do human joys like parties and weddings means to God? Watch Jesus at Levi's table or at the marriage in Cana and you will know. What about those barriers of prejudice and discrimination which we build to show our superiority over others? How does God feel about them? Look at Jesus as He smashes those barriers and stands with all despised ones. There is your answer. And how does

He feel even toward the straying, the spiteful, the rebellious, and the unlovely? Toward those who abuse their power, those who forget God? See Jesus weeping over wayward Jerusalem and you will know. But more than that, behold His unspeakable agony on Good Friday and yet the forgiving love with which He suffers for others. Then the deepest question of your life will be answered. *That* is how God feels about you!

The Apostle Paul spoke about "the light of the knowledge of the glory of God in the face of Christ (2 Cor. 4:6). What a way for the infinite, the almighty God, to make Himself known! Many years ago in a small, obscure corner of the world, a man walked among men and they saw His face—wet with the sweat of honest toil and bronzed by the sun. They saw how He looked at little children when He held them and how the tears ran down His cheeks at the death of a friend. They saw how He laughed at a banquet, how His cheeks flushed at the sight of hypocrisy and heartlessness, how He winced with terrible pain on a cross, how He beamed at the last shout, "It is finished." Later, with unspeakable joy they saw how He looked on Easter evening when He smiled, held up wounded hands and said, "Peace be with you." Some of those who saw all that testified, "We have beheld his glory, glory as of the only Son from the Father." They were saying, "He is the image and likeness of God. Here is God's supreme disclosure, His final word, all we know of God and all we need to know."

But apparently not everyone saw that. Even Philip, who had been with Jesus for three years, had not really seen it yet. With tenderness and mild rebuke, Jesus says to him, "Have I been with you so long, and yet you do not know me, Philip? How can you say, 'Show us the Father'? Don't you realize, even yet?"

It's easy to miss what's happening in the lives of those around us. There was an awkward, sassy girl in your neighborhood that you always thought of as a pain in the neck. As the years passed you didn't realize that she was becoming a lovely young lady, until one day her beauty took you by surprise and you noticed her for the first time. I was hardly aware of how fast one of our sons was growing until the day our eyes met on a level, and I knew he was becoming a man. We can fail to note the keen abilities developing in a young life or to appreciate the myriad little services of a loving mother. It's hard to see greatness up close to us. Sometimes we need to stand back and get a fresh look. I suppose there are people to whom the name Jesus is familiar, who know the parables He told and have heard the record of His life, who have glimpsed the kind of person He was, and who yet remain somewhat dulled by that familiarity. Maybe we are like that. The beauty, the uniqueness, the surpassing wonder of that life have somehow escaped us.

Do you really want to see God in a way that will satisfy your heart? Look then at Jesus Christ. Spend some time with one of the four gospels. Try to sweep from your mind old, secondhand impressions about Jesus and spend some time watching Him as He is pictured in the New Testament. Get a good look, a fresh look at the One who dared to say, "He who has seen me has seen the Father." Consider Him.

But looking — even watching — is not enough. There were some in Jesus' day who watched Him through narrowing eyes, intent on destroying Him. Some saw in Him nothing but a threat, a disturber, even a blasphemer. And there are people today, very familiar with the content of the New Testament, who yet have seen no vision of God. Looking is not enough. The spectator outlook won't do. Jesus says, "Believe me." "Believe me that I am in the Father and the Father in me; or else believe me for the sake of the works themselves." If we are to know Jesus, we need to believe the word that He speaks, to take Him seriously, to commit ourselves to what He commands, to launch out on what He promises. Why not respond now to whatever truth you find in Him? As you do that, you will begin to see

Him more and more clearly. And seeing Him, you will find what your heart most needs — the light of the knowledge of God's glory in the face of Jesus Christ.

QUESTIONS FOR DISCUSSION

1. What experiences in life have you found most deeply and permanently satisfying?

2. What would you say we can learn about God from observing the created order?

3. What common misconceptions of what God is like seem to vanish when we grasp that "God is like Jesus"?

4. In the light of these things, what special values do you see in a regular study of the four gospels?

19. A Second Source of Help

*"If you love me, you will keep my commandments.
And I will pray the Father, and he will give you another
Counselor, to be with you for ever, even the Spirit of
Truth, whom the world cannot receive, because it
neither sees him nor knows him; you know him, for he
dwells with you, and will be in you."*

(John 14:15-17)

SOME YEARS AGO, while I was in graduate school, I
was teaching a class in a nearby church on "Christian
Faith and Life." It was a stimulating group. We never
lacked for animated discussion. One evening when I
was beginning to deal with the subject of the Holy Spirit,
someone broke in suddenly. "I can understand about
God the Father, and the teachings of Jesus," she ex-
claimed, "but why do we have to have this Spirit?"

She was quite honest and forthright in her confusion
about the Holy Spirit. Since that time, I've often thought
that she speaks for a great many people, in the church
and out of it. Perhaps she speaks for you. Maybe the
Holy Ghost, to you, is scarcely more real and significant than the ghosts of folklore and superstition. You
may have wondered, perhaps without verbalizing it,
"Why do we have to have this Spirit?"

We preachers are partly at fault for this, I'm sure. We find it hard sometimes to preach and teach about the Holy Spirit. We can talk easily about God the Father, because everyone knows what a father is. Speaking of Jesus is even less a problem, because He lived a real human life here in this world. But how do you talk about a Spirit whose being is mysterious and whom no one has ever seen?

Some Christians, it's true, talk a great deal about the Spirit. They give the impression that they know all about Him — almost that they have Him at their disposal. They explain everything in their lives with reference to the Holy Spirit. Their enthusiasm is admirable, but they sometimes leave their fellow Christians somewhat puzzled. "Why don't I have all these experiences?" some are tempted to wonder. "Where did I miss out on all this?" Sometimes the whole subject is made to seem so strange, almost bizarre, that many tend to shrink back from it. They are ready to ask again, "Why do we have to have this Spirit?"

The best place to turn for an answer is to the words of Jesus Christ Himself. On the night before His crucifixion Jesus made this promise to His disciples: "I will pray the Father, and he will give you another Counselor." The whole conversation had centered, up to this point, around His going away. The disciples were troubled, heartsick at the thought. Jesus had assured them that He was going to prepare a place for His people and that one day He would come again to receive them. This was solid comfort, but it still left unanswered the question of how they would manage without Him until His return. He had told them that they would be able to do mighty works and that their prayers in His name would surely be heard, but they still found His leaving hard to accept. Now He promises that in His absence "another Counselor" will come to them. His word "another" did not mean "one of a different kind," but rather "a second one like the first." And the word translated "Counselor" literally means "one called

135

alongside to help": a guide, a comforter, a source of strength.

The counselor of the disciples up to this point had been Jesus Himself. He had been the One at their side to whom they looked for direction, on whom they could depend in time of need. Now in His absence they are to be given another Counselor *like Him*. The second One called alongside, this second source of help, is the Holy Spirit, the "Spirit of truth."

Now try to imagine what is was like for those disciples to have Jesus with them in Galilee and Judea. Suppose they had a weighty question on their minds. "What is God really like and what is He up to in the world?" Or, "How should I look at the things that are happening in our country today? What is God's perspective on them?" Or, "What would be the best thing, the right thing for me to do in this problem I am facing, this decision I have to make?" Now if Jesus was right there, they could talk to Him about it. Sometimes even that wasn't needed; they could tell by the expression on His face. I remember someone saying to me once, after a period of intense searching for God's will, that she felt like crying out, "Lord, I'd know how you feel about this if I could only come up and see your face!" But if Jesus was a guide and counselor at their side, He was also a marvelously strengthening companion. He had become to them not only Master and Teacher but also Friend. That friendship brought a new dimension into their lives. At our home we have a plaque on the bedroom wall that reads, "You came into my life and loved me, and somehow I became me." That's the way being with Jesus was for the disciples. His companionship affirmed them and called forth their own personhood. His strong caring warmed their lives, awakened new things within them, gave fresh meaning to what they did.

He was the One who buoyed them up and gave them courage. When they were with Him, nothing seemed impossible. In His presence they weren't afraid. They found they could begin to do things that had been beyond their abilities before.

Now Jesus tells them the Father will give them another companion. Someone else will be to them all that Jesus has been in the past: wisdom in their perplexity, companionship in their loneliness, strength in every time of weakness, courage and hope for each crisis of life. That is why the Spirit was to come.

Now what an amazing thing that is! Jesus Christ assures His followers that the Holy Spirit's coming will not only make up for His absence; it will actually be better for them than His remaining with them in the flesh! Later on in the conversation He puts it just that way: "It is to your advantage that I go away, for if I do not go away, the Counselor will not come to you; but if I go, I will send him to you" (John 16:7). How could anything possibly be better, we ask, than having the physical presence of Jesus Christ with us?

For one thing, the Spirit's companionship will be permanent. "He will be with you," says Jesus, "forever." No accident of circumstance, no distance of miles can ever separate believers from their source of help in the Spirit. Wherever they go, whatever they suffer, no matter what happens in this world the Counselor will be there.

But more than that, His presence will be an inward reality. That is the richest, most gladdening part of Jesus' promise. The other Counselor will be not only *with* the disciples but *in* them. If it is a great thing to have Christ living *with* us, what would it mean to have His own Spirit living *within* us? And that's what the coming of the Counselor means. That is the wonder of His ministry. He brings the presence of the living Christ to our inmost lives. Now the whole picture is opening before us: Jesus must depart from us in the flesh so that He can be with us by the Spirit. He must leave His place by our side so that He can take up His abode in our hearts. Now His living presence can be not only an example and pattern "out there," but new power transforming our lives from within.

Remember how, even after three years spent with Him, the disciples were still so weak, so dull of understanding, so prone to fall in the time of testing? Even though they had walked with Him in close companionship, they were thoroughly demoralized, fearful, and helpless after the crucifixion. But think of the contrast some weeks later. The presence of Jesus had now become a life-changing reality within them. It was actually His life now being lived out in theirs.

Ponder what that means. You've read about the American chess wizard, Bobby Fischer. Suppose now for a moment, those of you who know something about the game of chess, that somehow Bobby Fischer could live inside you so that his amazing knowledge of the game, his incomparable skill, could be employed in the moves you make. Or imagine once more that the spirit of a musician like Beethoven lived in you so that his fantastic gift of conceiving and creating melody could find fresh expression through you. Now those things, of course, aren't possible. But what if Jesus Christ the Lord, the supreme Master of the art of living, of loving, of serving — suppose that He could dwell in you by His Spirit. That *is* possible, that is *actual,* in the lives of millions of people today.

We can begin to see how that works in any close human relationship. Persons with whom we live, especially those whom we love and admire, impart something to our lives. Their influence, like some hidden river, flows into us, making us different, molding our ideals and our ways of looking at life. And in a far more profound way, by the gift of His Holy Spirit, Jesus Christ lives His risen life in and through us.

How vital it is to recognize this close relationship between Christ Himself and the ministry of the Holy Spirit! If the whole subject of the Spirit seems vague and hazy to us, there may be a certain haziness about our relationship to Jesus Christ. Be sure of this: we will never know the Holy Spirit apart from personal commitment to Christ. Jesus says about the Spirit, that the world cannot receive Him "because it neither sees him nor knows him." To those who have no place for God in their lives, all talk about the Holy Spirit seems nonsense. Without a living faith we have no capacity even to perceive the presence and work of the Spirit. The disciples, on the other hand, are said to know the Spirit because He "dwells with them." They know Him because they have seen Him at work in Jesus, their Master.

For us, too, trust in Christ as Lord, commitment to Him, comes first. Only then can the Spirit's work be experienced and understood. Notice again what came before Jesus' promise about the Spirit's coming: "If you love me you will keep my commandments. And I will pray the Father, and he will give you another Counselor." Everything starts with believing in Jesus, as He constantly insists. When we believe in Him and in His saving love, we begin to love Him in response. And that love is not merely a sentiment; we express it by obeying His commands. It is to such disciples, followers who trust and love and obey Him, that the Savior promises the gift of the Spirit.

Let's never forget that. The Holy Spirit is not a kind of power that we can turn on and off at will. Nor is He a source of spiritual experiences that we can tap if we only have the right formula. He is the Spirit of the risen Lord and the work He comes to do is inseparable from the work which Jesus Christ has already done. If we want to know Him more fully, it will be along the path of trust in Christ and loving obedience to His will. As we seek to trust and obey, we shall find that the other Counselor is always present, helping us all the way. If today you trust in Jesus Christ, you can be sure that the Holy Spirit is living in you. Thank Him for that.

And if, trusting Christ, you love Him and want to obey His will, making Him known in the world, then be assured that the help you need will be given. That's why you have the Spirit.

QUESTIONS FOR DISCUSSION

1. Why is it difficult to understand the doctrine of the Holy Spirit?

2. How is the Holy Spirit's ministry like that of Jesus?

3. In what ways was it advantageous for the disciples (and for us) that Jesus should return to the Father?

4. How is commitment to Christ related to our experience of the Holy Spirit?

20. The Secret of Fruitfulness

"I am the true vine, and my Father is the vinedresser. Every branch of mine that bears no fruit, he takes away, and every branch that does bear fruit he prunes, that it may bear more fruit. You are already made clean by the word which I have spoken to you. Abide in me, and I in you. As the branch cannot bear fruit by itself, unless it abides in the vine, neither can you, unless you abide in me. I am the vine, you are the branches. He who abides in me, and I in him, he it is that bears much fruit, for apart from me you can do nothing."

(John 15:1-5)

WE ALL WANT our lives to accomplish something, don't we? Each of us seems to long — sometimes almost desperately — to be a truly significant person in this world. We want to know that it has made some difference that we have lived, that we have made a contribution while we were here. We need to feel that we have counted for something. Nothing is quite so chilling and bleak as the fear that our lives do not really matter, that they have no importance either to ourselves or to others.

I was talking to a young man about this recently. He told of the intolerable craving he had to be an influential person, to have some effect on the people around

141

him. When it seemed that he was unable to touch or move the lives of others, it was hard to fight off a feeling of meaninglessness. Some, I am sure, feel this more keenly than others. Not everyone burns with a passion to change the world. But I wonder if anyone is really content to be a nobody. Somerset Maugham, in a poignant passage, once described a group of "old people who lived their days away, and when they died, it was as though they had never been." Who wouldn't shrink from the thought of living a whole life like that?

But isn't it a kind of forlorn hope, an empty dream, that the average person can accomplish anything very significant? Who is one person among billions of others, especially if he is limited in gifts and opportunities? Perhaps a few people in every age can make an impression — those with outstanding genius or wealth or power — but isn't that too much to expect for typical taxpayers like us? It's perhaps that feeling of powerlessness, that smothering sense of being irrelevant, that sometimes drives people into bizarre, destructive behavior. Every now and then we read of someone who committed a horrible crime because he wanted to get his name in the papers, wanted to show that he was someone. The hijacker, the arsonist, the assassin — all may be pushed on by the same motives. Anything to get myself noticed, to make people see that I'm someone to be reckoned with. After all, our society seems to award the greatest publicity to the most monstrous evils.

That raises the question sharply, doesn't it, as to what really constitutes a significant human life? Is it the degree of notoriety we achieve? Is it the number of people whose lives we influence? Is it the creative work we leave behind us? Are the newspaper editors and the historians the ones who finally decide which human lives are most productive and worthwhile? Or is there another way to look at this whole question? I believe that there is.

It was said of Jesus Christ that he "knew what was in man." He knew our dreadful potential for evil and also our higher capacities. He knew also how much we want our lives to count. Toward the end of His own life here on earth He spoke of how He had finished the work which had been given Him to do, and He finally breathed His last with the triumphant shout, "It is accomplished!" He knew what it meant to live a significant, productive life. In fact, He told His followers just how it could be done.

According to Jesus, the secret of fruitfulness lies in our relationship to Him. Negatively, He stated it like this: "apart from me you can do nothing." That surely is one of His most daring claims. Without Him, without a vital relationship to Him, without the resources He provides, our lives remain barren and unproductive. How do we handle a statement like that? What of the great conquerors of history who paid no allegiance to Jesus Christ? What of the many gifted artists who never even knew His name? Are we to believe that all the products of human skill and inventiveness, all the great achievements of man's hand and brain count for nothing at all? Are the labors of a scientist with his test tubes or an Einstein with his equations of no value simply because these individuals do not acknowledge Jesus as the Christ? "Surely," someone objects, "Jesus has overstated Himself here."

It is doubtful, though, if Jesus ever intended to play down or negate these varied kinds of human accomplishment. He is saying, however, that many of the things that we regard as significant are seen differently from the Lord's perspective. With Jesus, it is a question of what is significant for God's purposes, what has lasting value in His eyes. And Jesus claims that, apart from Him, none of the fruit which God prizes and for which He looks is brought forth in our lives.

His meaning becomes clearer as we study this beautiful analogy of the vine and the branches. It was a figure of speech familiar to the people of Israel. God through His prophets, had often spoken of Israel as His vine, His pleasant plant. Israel was planted by God, as it were, in the hope that she would bring forth the good fruit of faithful worship and loving obedience. All too often, however, the cherished vine seemed to bring forth worthless fruit. The people were unresponsive to God's purpose for them. They rebelled against Him and went their own way. Idolatry and transgression — this was all the vine seemed capable of producing.

So Jesus' word, "I am the true vine," carried a pointed message for Israel. What the chosen people had failed to be, He was. In Jesus Christ God had begun a new community within the old. He had planted a new vine on earth, destined to bring forth good fruit.

But now the analogy is given a wealth of new meaning. Jesus says to His followers, "I am the vine; you are the branches." Picture in your mind's eye a giant grapevine, spreading out over its wooden supports, seeming to blanket a whole hillside. From the massive central stock to the most distant, tiny tendril, the whole vine pulses with one common life. Each branch draws its sustenance, its power to bring forth fruit, from the vine to which it is joined. A vital, fruit-bearing branch without the vine is inconceivable. Severed from the vine, it can expect only barrenness and death. Everything depends on vital contact with the vine.

Jesus is speaking here about the central reality of the Christian faith: the union of His people with Himself. He has already told the disciples that He is soon to go away and that the Holy Spirit, the other Comforter, will come to dwell in their lives. What He now says about the vine and the branches opens up the full significance of the Spirit's ministry. The great work of the Holy Spirit is to bring us into a living, personal relationship with Jesus Christ. He, the Spirit, brings the life of the risen, glorified Jesus into the experience of each disciple. If Christ is the reservoir of living water, then the Holy Spirit is the channel through whom that living water reaches us. If Christ is the source of power, then it is the Holy Spirit who makes the connection with our otherwise powerless lives. The New Testament itself abounds with images of this union with the Savior. Those who believe in Him are said to be "members of Christ's body." They are "living stones" in the temple of God, built upon Him, the chief cornerstone. The union between Christ and His people is even compared to the marriage bond. The closest of human ties are used and transcended in describing this marvelous gift. Christ, the true vine, imparts His own life to us who are the branches. It is then that our lives can truly bear fruit.

The nature of this fruit becomes clear when we understand the analogy. "Fruit" here refers to what Christ Himself brings forth through us, that which His own life in us produces. In the character of a Christian, fruit means likeness to Christ, what Paul describes as the fruit of the Spirit: love, joy, peace, long-suffering, gentleness, goodness, meekness, self-control, faithfulness. In terms of activity, fruit means the kind of action and ministry that characterized the life of Jesus Himself. "Greater works than these will he do," He promised (John 14:12). It means walking as He walked, serving as He served. But for Him fruit means even more; it means the communication of His life to others. It is not only production but reproduction: the bringing of other human lives into vital contact with His life. To be a fruitful Christian means both to express Christ's life and to share it with others. And if we are to do that, Jesus tells us that one thing is absolutely essential: we must *abide* in Him.

What does it mean to abide in Jesus Christ? Some Christians, profoundly impressed by this image of the vine and the branches, have seen this abiding to involve little more than what the branch does to remain in the vine: passive acceptance, total dependence. To abide in Christ means simply to allow His life to be our life. Or, as the familiar phrase puts it, to "let go and let God."

There are others, however, who see this passage quite differently. They notice how much Jesus says in the context about obedience to His commands. To them, one abides in Christ by diligently striving to do God's will. On this view, abiding comes as a result of our earnest religious effort. For some, then, abiding is a passive resting; for others it is an active doing.

Both the words of Jesus and the experience of Christians testify that these two elements really belong together. The Apostle John in his first letter gives us added insight about the meaning of Jesus' "commandment." "And this is his commandment," he writes, "that we should believe in the name of his Son Jesus Christ and love one another, just as he has commanded us. All who keep his commandments abide in him, and he in them" (1 John 3:23). Here it is stated again that abiding means keeping His commandments, and included among those is faith in Jesus Christ, God's Son. Abiding in Christ seems to carry this twofold meaning — faith in Jesus and love for others. Jesus' call to abide in Him as branches in the vine means the sustaining and developing of a twofold relationship. We need to deepen our relationship with God in Christ by worship, prayer, Bible study, and a believing openness to His life and strength. And we need also to express that relationship horizontally in our dealings with others, acting toward them in Christ's love. We are to be constantly receiving from Christ in faith and sharing with others in love. That is the rhythm of Christian living. That is what it means to abide in Christ and that, in His view, is a truly productive life. It depends little, if at all, on talent or position, on drive or aggressiveness. It is a present possibility for each one of us. You can begin living it right now by opening your life in faith to Jesus as Savior and committing yourself to His lordship. Those who do that, and who continue in the way, have really found the secret of fruitfulness.

Oh, believe that, won't you? You *are* a significant person. And you *can* make a great contribution in this world. Look toward Christ. Believe on Him. Abide in Him, and you will live the life that counts.

1. What makes a human life truly significant?

2. What other images or comparisons (besides the vine and the branches) are used in the New Testament to describe our union with Christ?

3. What is the nature of the fruit we are called upon to bear?

4. What is involved, on our part, if we are to "abide in Christ"?

21. His One Command

"As the Father has loved me, so have I loved you;
abide in my love. If you keep my commandments, you
will abide in my love, just as I have kept my Father's
commandments and abide in his love. These things I
have spoken to you, that my joy may be in you, and
that your joy may be full."

(John 15:10, 11)

DID YOU KNOW that Jesus gave His disciples only one
command? He taught them a great deal, of course, and
gave them many indications of His will for their lives,
but He left them with only one charge which He
described as His "commandment." Sometimes He said
"This is my commandment." At other times he called
it "a new commandment," but the substance was always
the same. Even when He spoke of "commandments" in
the plural, saying, "These things I command you," all
were resolved into one. This was it: "That you love
one another."

Now there is something remarkable about this. Picture the scene in which Jesus was speaking these words.
He knows that rejection, agony, and death are ahead
for Him. The dreadful prospects of Gethsemane and
Golgotha are vividly before His mind. But strangely,

He is not preoccupied or moody. His thoughts are with His followers, with their needs and their future. Incredibly, He stoops to wash their feet. Quietly, cheerfully, He moves from one disciple to the next, performing the lowly service which these men had been too proud or thoughtless to assume. They had been quarreling, it seems, about who was to be the greatest in the kingdom of heaven; so He showed them afresh how He felt about them and gave them an unforgettable pattern of loving service.

Now, the foot-washing ended, Jesus speaks to them at some length. He tells them of His departure to be with the Father, of the Holy Spirit's coming, of the great works that will soon be theirs to do, and of the bitter opposition they will face. But through all that He says, coming back again and again like a refrain, are these words, "That you love one another."

Why all this emphasis on mutual love? Obviously the disciples needed it. But there must have been so many other things they needed, too. They had an awesome responsibility before them, a worldwide task. Where would they begin? What would be their strategy? How would they organize? Important as those questions were, this other matter seemed in our Lord's eyes to claim priority. He wanted them to learn, above everything else, how to love each other. Why was He so insistent on that?

As we study Jesus' last words to His disciples we begin to understand at least some of the reasons for this emphasis. For one thing, Christ makes it plain that we cannot be near to Him if we do not love our Christian brethren. The disciples could not be alienated from each other and still stay in close touch with Him. They had lived for almost three years in His companionship. Now He was going away but He promised to be with them still in the person of the indwelling Holy Spirit. They would be united to Him as branches in the vine, drawing all their life and sustenance from His risen life. But to be joined to Him, to share His life, meant to be united to the other branches as well. There was no avoiding the connection: if they were close to Him they would be close to each other. If they were distant from their brethren they would be far from Christ. To reject them meant to reject Him. To injure them, God forbid, was to wound His heart. As John Calvin once put it vividly: "He who hurts his fellow Christian tears Jesus Christ in pieces."

Jesus had called these men His "friends." They were no longer servants now, but men close to His heart, understanding His mind, sympathizing with His purpose. But those other disciples, each one of them, were His friends as well. There was Peter — headstrong, impulsive, speaking before he thought. There was Thomas — inclined to look on the dark side of things. Then there were James with his volatile temper and Matthew with a questionable past. Yes, Jesus called them all as His friends, and anyone who wanted His company had to welcome them, too.

Some years ago one of our sons was asked to join a club. Unfortunately, it was one of those clubs that are designed as much to keep certain people out as to have certain others in. And though the members of the club wanted our son to join, they were not inviting his best buddy, with whom he spent most of his time. We talked together about how he should handle that request. He finally decided to suggest a package deal to the club. "If you want me, you want my friend, too." And isn't that what Christ says to all who express interest in following Him? "If you want Me you want My friends."

Jesus even teaches that a practical love for our fellow Christians leads us to know *Him* better. Listen: "He who has my commandments" — and we've seen what those are — "He who has my commandments and keeps them, he it is who loves me; and he who loves me will be loved by my Father, and I will love him and manifest myself to him" (John 14:21). If Christ, then, is not real to us, at least one of the reasons may be our failure or refusal to love some of His people.

One thing is sure: to have Christ in your heart means that you have a place for His followers there, too.

But there is more involved even than that. Jesus implied that we cannot live a full and happy life as Christians if we do not love our brethren. After reminding them to keep His commandment of love, He adds this: "These things I have spoken to you, that my joy may be in you, and that your joy may be full." Have you ever thought of the fact that love is the secret of joy? When Paul lists the fruit of the Spirit in Galatians 5 he mentions love first and joy next. There is meaning in that sequence. I would venture to say that the most happy people are those who care most about those around them. And, on the other hand, I would guess that the most bored and discontented ones among us are those who have been living in a self-centered way.

You know how it works. You're lying in bed at night and the baby cries. You don't feel like getting up. Maybe if you pretend that you're still asleep your wife (or your husband) will get up and see what's the matter. But this time you struggle with yourself and because you know your spouse is tired you get up and do what has to be done. When you finally get back in bed you may feel weary but you also feel good. You're glad because, somehow, your caring won out over your self-saving and you were able to act in love.

Or maybe in your case you'd been nursing a grudge for a long time, feeling pretty miserable inside along with it. Finally you realized how foolish and fruitless that all was and you reached out with a generous heart to the person who had wronged you. Things got straightened out. And how light-hearted you felt all of a sudden!

Why does Christ call His people to love each other? Not just because God happens to like that kind of behavior but because it's the way of abundant life. Do you want prayer to be meaningful and rich? Listen to His word: "If you abide in me, and my words abide in you, ask whatever you will, and it shall be done for you" (John 15:7). When we don't forgive a brother or when a relationship with someone in our family goes sour, our prayers are hindered, short-circuited. The sense of God's presence gets dim and the assurance of being heard fades away. You simply can't pray if you don't love. In fact, you can't do much of anything. Jesus says if you don't abide in His love by loving your brethren, then your life amounts to a big zero. If you're loveless you may keep on existing but it can hardly be said that you really live. Christ wants His crowning joy to be in our lives, the joy He knew in a life of self-giving love. But we can't have it if we close our hearts to the people around us. Oh, that we could see that more clearly!

There is one more key reason why Jesus was so concerned about mutual love among His followers. This had to do with the whole success of their mission in the world. He made it plain that without loving hearts, they could never be His witnesses. Christ sent them, we remember, to bear fruit: not only the fruit of Christian character, but also a harvest of redeemed lives, converts led to a knowledge of the Savior. An essential element in the whole program would be their love for each other. "By this," said Jesus, "all men will know that you are my disciples, if you have love for one another" (John 13:35). That's how people will recognize that we belong to Christ. That's how they will come to recognize Him.

This is the forgotten factor, I'm afraid, in many evangelism programs. I'm all for those programs, by the way — 100 percent. Let's be made all things to all men, that by all means we may save some. Let's lay hold of every medium and make us of each opportunity to bring the Gospel of Christ to every person in the world. But let's never forget that no matter how aggressive we are in our evangelistic efforts, sooner or later we need to bring these inquirers, these new converts, into a fellowship of Christians. And there, the quality of life in that congregation will either powerfully reinforce our witness or it may practically destroy it.

Let's be aware of it — the world around us is skeptical. Many people are hard to impress. Talk about a loving Savior sometimes fails to get a hearing because the ones who profess to be saved don't love very much. A man in India once told Billy Graham, "I would be a Christian if I could see one." We don't know how faithful he would have been to that bargain, but maybe that's what many people around us are saying deep down inside. "If I could only see this love of God in action in the lives of people in the church, then I'd take a second look."

You know, it really works that way. I know of congregations, and you probably do too, where the love of Christians for each other has a magnetic winsomeness about it. Those outside see how they care about each other, how they enjoy being together, how an accepting love shines out from them. And how attractive that looks! Who wouldn't want to be part of a group like that? Who wouldn't be eager to know their secret? I believe people are hungry for a fellowship like that. They see enough of backbiting, pettiness, of rejection and coldness all around them. They'll never be won by a church which simply demonstrates more of the same. But let Christians care deeply about each other and witness from within that kind of warmth, and other people are going to discover new life.

Well, if loving our fellow Christians is all that important to Jesus Christ, then what ought we to do about it? First of all, let's adopt His priorities. Let's emphasize what He did. Let's not be content with flawless orthodoxy or with vigorous social action if either of those is a substitute for loving our fellow Christians. Let's not assume that anything can take the place of that.

Then there's this practical hint. If you have trouble loving people, begin to act toward them as if you did love them. You don't have to start with warm feelings. Just start treating them as though you really did care about them and see what happens. It's a kind of law of human nature that when you treat people badly you like them even less, but when you begin to act toward them in a kindly way your feelings and attitudes may well warm up, too.

But most of all, if you really want to love your fellow Christian, dwell much on the Lord's love for you. Remember how kind and merciful, how unbelievably patient. He has been with you. Remember how He gave Himself up for you. Open your life more and more to that love and that Lord, and you will find it increasingly easy to love His people, too. And you will be obeying with a glad and grateful heart His "one command."

QUESTIONS FOR DISCUSSION

1. What did Jesus mean when He called His disciples not servants but friends?

2. What else besides careful Bible study is involved in a growing knowledge of Christ?

3. What are the qualities of life within a congregation which most make others want to be a part of it?

4. What practical steps can we take to become more loving persons?

22. Chosen for a Mission

"No longer do I call you servants, for the servant does not know what his master is doing; but I have called you friends, for all that I have heard from my Father I have made known to you. You did not choose me, but I chose you and appointed you that you should go and bear fruit and that your fruit should abide; so that whatever you ask the Father in my name, he may give it to you."

(John 15:15, 16)

Do YOU EVER feel like a nobody? You are only one among billions. Perhaps you have no outstanding talents to set you apart from others. In fact, the circle of people who know anything at all about you is quite small. It's easy to feel, isn't it, that you don't matter very much?

Are you really, come to think of it, of special value to anyone else? You realize that the world would go on in much the same way without you. People would get along if you weren't around. Things wouldn't be appreciably different. It's painful to face, but you're not indispensable. What you do could probably be done by someone else. And so you wonder if your life has any particular meaning. Like everyone else, you're born, you go through the struggles of growing up. You work at earning a living, you worry over what's happening in the world. As the years pass, your health begins to fail. You battle against old age and infirmity and you finally succumb. And all along the road until that point, life has its frustrations and its disappointments. On bad days you sometimes wonder if the whole thing is worth it. You wonder if your life counts for anything.

If this touches a responsive chord in you, you're not alone; you have lots of company. Remember Willy Loman, the pathetic figure in Arthur Miller's *Death of a Salesman?* It was said of him that "he never knew who he was." He always felt "kind of temporary" about himself. An aging baseball player quit the Los Angeles Dodgers several years ago for a chance to play in Japan. He gave this for his reason to inquiring newsmen: "I can't stand being a nobody." All of us find that hard. To some, feeling like a "nobody" becomes painfully destructive. Our mental institutions are filled with people who have been squelched by life, convinced that they are unimportant, finding no value or meaning in their lives. I suppose there have always been those who feel this way, but the problem seems to be particularly acute in our time. This age of mass production, of booming population, of fantastic technology and automation has had a depersonalizing effect on all of us. It's harder than ever these days to feel that you're "somebody."

How can the situation be helped? There is a rising school of psychotherapy today which claims that we cannot help mental patients toward wholeness unless we can give them some content for their lives — an aim and purpose for their existence. In other words, they need at least to see a task before them. It is all the more helpful when they seem especially fitted for the task; when it constitutes for them a *mission*. To know that he has a mission makes a person feel significant and gives his life the value of uniqueness.

I don't know whether this holds true for everyone.

It was certainly true for me. As a teenager, groping for a sense of identity, wanting passionately to be someone significant, searching for meaning in my life, I came to know Jesus Christ in a personal way. Soon after that, although I don't remember exactly how, these words of Christ began to exert a profound influence on my life: "You did not choose me, but I chose you and appointed you that you should go and bear fruit and that your fruit should abide." I learned that I had been chosen, chosen for a mission.

Most Americans have become familiar in recent years with what happens on the television program "Mission Impossible." In some obscure, exotic place Jim Phelps receives notice of an assignment, a mission of great difficulty, involving many dangers. His next step is to select a task force of persons especially equipped for the mission. Slowly, thoughtfully, he sorts through pictures of possible candidates and chooses a few of them. Here, of course, the choice is made because of their unusual skill or insight or strength. These are top-notch people who can do exciting things. You get the feeling that they could be successful in any line of work.

In marked contrast, this word of Jesus about a mission comes to very ordinary people, those who often feel they don't amount to much. And what a difference it can make in their lives!

There are three things about this mission that make life deeply significant for those who receive it. The first has to do with the One who issues the call. To be chosen for a task is an honor in proportion to the greatness of the one who appoints us. To be chosen for any football all-star team would be a mark of distinction; but if a super-coach like the late Vince Lombardi selected you, the honor would be especially great. Suppose the greatest conductor in the world invited you to play in his orchestra, or suppose a genius like Einstein wanted you for an understudy. How would you feel about that? Well think, then, of what it means that Jesus Christ, the Son of God, the Lord of everything, says to each of His followers, "I chose you. I selected you. I wanted you for My mission."

In this act of choosing, Christ calls us into a special relationship with Himself. Listen to this word: "No longer do I call you servants, for the servant does not know what the master is doing; but I have called you friends, for all that I have heard from my Father I have made known to you." Sometimes people are sent on a mission about which they know very little. They are assigned a specific task, but they have no inkling as to the overall strategy of which it is a part. Their skills may be valued, but they are not personally trusted. They are not "in on" the larger plans of the one who chooses them. But those whom Christ selects become His friends. He shows them what He is up to. He shares with them His grand design. He reveals to them what is in His heart.

Could anything impart more meaning to life than this? We are fellow laborers with the Lord of glory, honored participants in the purpose for which the world was made. None are hirelings in this service; all have been taken into the confidence of the King.

Jesus seems to lay special emphasis on the fact that we did not choose Him. But was that really true? Hadn't these disciples responded to His call? Hadn't they left all to follow Him? They had remained true when others had turned away. They had promised to stand by Him no matter what came. Couldn't you call that a choice on their part? Yes, that was all true; but behind their commitment lay His summons, His invitation. Christ always took the initiative. He came to people where they were, in their familiar surroundings, in the midst of their work and relationships, and called them from that point to follow Him. The gospels emphasize repeatedly that it is Christ who chooses those who come after Him. He knows them; He sees them, even before they respond.

So if today you feel any inclination to follow Jesus Christ, any purpose of heart to serve Him, you can be

sure that His prior call lies behind it. There's a great
hymn that puts it this way,

> I sought the Lord and afterward I knew
> He moved my soul to seek Him, seeking me.
> It was not I who found, O Savior true;
> No, I was found of Thee.

> I find, I walk, I love, but oh, the whole
> Of love is but my answer, Lord, to Thee.
> For Thou wast long beforehand with my soul.
> Always thou lovedst me.

If that be true, if Christ has loved us and claimed us in
advance for His purpose, how can we ever think lightly
or cheaply of ourselves again?

But we are not only called by a great Lord; we are
also given a tremendously significant mission. "I appointed you," said Jesus, "that you should go and bear
fruit." He had been speaking earlier of himself as the
"vine" and His followers as "branches" who must
remain in touch with Him to bear fruit. There the fruit
of Christian character was chiefly in view, the expressions in our daily behavior of Christ's own life — lived
out in us. That kind of fruit, believers can bring forth
anywhere, at any time, because they are united with
their Lord. But here Jesus speaks of a fruit that we
are to *go* and bear. That word "go" points unmistak-
ably to our task of bringing the Gospel to all peoples.
Christians are chosen to make Christ known, to be the
instruments through whom His salvation is communicated to others. "Fruit" here means the expression and
extension of life. It means Christians producing other
Christians by their witness in deed and word. We are
chosen to be instruments in bringing others to true
humanness, to abundant life in Christ. What a task!

The important thing to remember is that this mission
is not confined to clergymen, missionaries, and evan-
gelists. Jesus is saying that the mission of every one
of His servants, whatever their occupation may be, has

to do with *people*. Whatever your daily work, your real vocation is a ministry to persons. Yours is the greatest task that could be committed to anyone: to pass along what you have received, to share Christ with others, to love them in His name. And that you can do in the home or in the marketplace, in the office or the shop, on a ball field or in a rest home. Wherever there are people whom God loves and for whom Christ died, there is your high mission. You are chosen to be His person for them.

There is one more word of vast encouragement here. Not only are we chosen by the King and given a glorious mission, but we are assured of its lasting results. Jesus has appointed us that we should go and bear fruit and that our fruit should *remain*. All of us want to contribute something lasting while we live here: some work of art, some memorial award, some building that bears our name, some monument to our achievement, anything to feel that what we have done in life has not been completely lost. When we pour our efforts into something, when we give to some task our life's blood, as it were, we long to know that it will still be there when we're gone. Otherwise the labor of our lives seems to lose its meaning. Here Jesus Christ assures us that the fruit we bear in a loving witness and ministry to those around us will never pass away. All other creations and accomplishments are transient, fleeting, compared to this. When we make it our aim to see Christ formed in others, placing ourselves at His disposal for their sakes, the toil of our lives will still endure when everything else has crumbled into dust. What you impart to another in Christ's name will never fade away.

So take heart today, whoever you are, whatever your situation, in this word of the Gospel. Jesus Christ is calling you to trust Him, to commit yourself to Him as the one who died and rose again for you, who lives forever to be your Savior. And as you trust Him, you can know with deep assurance that your life has value and meaning; for He calls you to share with Him in a great work and promises that your labor will never be in vain. "You did not choose me," He says, "but I chose you and appointed you that you should go and bear fruit and that your fruit should abide."

QUESTIONS FOR DISCUSSION

1. What would you most like to be remembered for?

2. What is there about having a life-purpose which makes us feel good about ourselves?

3. In what sense do we choose Christ, and in what sense does He choose us?

4. What special encouragement about our work comes from being chosen for it by the Lord?

23. Conquering the World

"The hour is coming, indeed it has come, when you will be scattered, every man to his home, and will leave me alone; yet I am not alone, for the Father is with me. I have said this to you, that in me you may have peace. In the world you have tribulation; but be of good cheer, I have overcome the world."

(John 16:32, 33)

LET ME CHECK your knowledge of history just once. Here's the question: What great ruler is reported to have said, "I have conquered the world"? Was it Alexander the Great, after he had completed his phenomenal conquest of the Persian empire? No. Some historians say that Alexander had dreams of world conquest and aspired to be worshiped as a god, but he never made the claim that he had achieved it. Was it Julius Caesar then? Wasn't he supposed to have coined that gem of a sentence, familiar to all Latin students, *Veni, vidi, vici* — "I came, I saw, I conquered"? Well, even if he did, he was speaking of a territory much more modest and less extensive than the whole world. Or was it Napoleon when he was about to bring all Europe to its knees? Or Hitler after Dunkirk, when he seemed on the verge of winning World War II? No, none of these. There have been leaders, ancient and modern, who boasted that they would win universal dominion, as well as heavyweight boxing champions who were sure they could lick anyone alive. But not one of them, so far as I know, ever publicly announced that he had subdued the world.

We have it on the best authority, however, that one person has made that claim. According to John the apostle, one of Jesus' closest friends, these were our Lord's exact words: "I have conquered the world."

Now the circumstances under which Jesus said this made it all the more remarkable. At the time, it wasn't apparent that He had conquered much of anything. Far from being a world ruler, He owned no real estate at all. By His own admission, He had not even a place to lay His head. He commanded no army. In fact, it was only a handful of men and a few women who continued to take His leadership seriously. And most of them were soon to leave Him and run away. You could hardly say that He had captured even the *attention* of the world, since He lived among a subject people in a tiny country and was virtually unknown outside its borders. Many of those who did hear His teaching either rejected it outright or failed to understand it.

What made His claim most shocking, however, was that He spoke it with clear-eyed knowledge that He was about to be arrested, humiliated, and killed. And if He had expected some popular movement to rise in His favor, He was soon to be disappointed. The fickle crowds, when faced with a choice, rejected Him and chose instead to have Barabbas, a revolutionary, released to them. Still, looking forward to what seemed like certain disgrace, defeat, and death, Jesus claimed to have conquered the world.

Is there anything we can take seriously about that announcement? Or does it simply sound like the exiled Napoleon on the little island of St. Helena, speaking pathetically at the close of life about the great things

163

he might have done? What can Jesus mean by the strange announcement that He has already overcome the world?

Obviously He has something in mind quite different from what we normally understand by those words. "To conquer the world" in ordinary speech means to defeat all opposing forces, to gain control over all the world's power structures, and to exercise authority over all its peoples. To say the least, it wasn't evident that Jesus had come close to doing any of those things.

We get our first clue to His meaning when we understand how He uses that term "world." Sometimes in the Bible the word "world" means this planet earth, or the earth in its larger setting amid the starry heavens. At other times it may mean the people in the world, as in that favorite of all Bible verses, "For God so loved the world that he gave his only Son." On the lips of Jesus, however, the word most frequently has a negative cast to it. He seems to speak of "the world" as a vast system in opposition to God, to His Son, and to His servants. Listen to these words of Jesus: "The world . . . hates me because I testify of it that its works are evil" (John 7:7). "If the world hates you," He said to His disciples, "know that it has hated me before it hated you." The disciples, we learn, will weep and lament when Jesus is taken from them, but "the world will rejoice." As the Apostle John explains more fully in one of his letters, "the world" stands for all in human life that resists God's will, rebels against His authority, and sets itself up in vaunted independence from Him. "The world," you might say, is almost personalized here as God's great rival for the allegiance and affection of mankind. John cautions his fellow Christians, accordingly, not to love the world or the things in the world. "If anyone loves the world," he continues, "love for the Father is not in him. For all that is in the world, the lust of the flesh, and the lust of the eyes and the pride of life, is not of the Father but is of the world" (1 John 2:15, 16). The world is the

164

sum total of human society with all its drives and powers, its civilization and culture, as those operate in willful disregard of the creator. "The world" is a kind of power structure which denies and defies God's lordship over all of life.

Now it is this vast world system, this prevailing spirit of the age, which Jesus claims to have conquered. The decisive battle had been fought, and won. The world had tried to intimidate Him with its sneers, its taunts, its threats. It was about to arrest Him, to put Him on trial, to condemn and crucify Him. It was out to thwart and destroy His divine mission here on earth. By turns, the world had tried another tactic, seeking to beguile Him with its allurements. It had promised Him dominion, fame, security, satisfaction, if only He would turn aside from God's appointed path. But neither its threats nor its blandishments had moved Him. He had remained faithful to God in the midst of all these pressures. He had resisted to the very end. In that sense, He had conquered. He did not capitulate; He never gave in; He overcame the world.

Now notice that He spoke this as a word of strong encouragement to His followers. "Be of good cheer, I have overcome the world." These men needed encouragement in the worst way. Jesus might have overcome the world, but pressures seemed to be too much for them. They had just been told that, in spite of their professions of loyalty, they would soon abandon Him in His hour of distress. They would be cowed by the world's blustering and enticed by its promises of personal safety and security. They hardly felt like conquerors.

What is more, Jesus told them quite pointedly what was ahead for them. "In the world you have tribulation." I suppose that every one of us can testify in some way to the truth of that. This world is a place of troubles for us all. It is a world of sickness and pain, of frustration and disappointment, of sorrow and death. There are few of us who at some point in life cannot identify with the word of Scripture that "man is born to trouble as the sparks fly upward" (Job 5:7).

Yes, we can agree with Jesus that in the world we have tribulation, but when He speaks here to His disciples it is also about trouble of a special kind: the difficulties that come upon people because they belong to God and seek to do His will here on earth. Those who seem "different" are always suspect and seem to generate antagonism. Let those of another race or nation, of a different culture and upbringing, of a foreign language or life style, move into a neighborhood and opposition of some kind is almost certain to arise. This will be most radically true, says Jesus, in the case of those who seek first God's kingdom and His righteousness. Their aim is different from the prevailing aims of this world. Their loyalties, their values, come from Him rather than from the culture around them. They are out of step with the world. They march to a different drum. And because of that they have tribulation.

This is not merely an academic subject or a problem peculiar to the first-century Christians. Let any man or woman today espouse an unpopular cause, or defend an oppressed minority and the pressures will be there. Let a voice be raised that calls injustice or discrimination by its real name and resistance will form. Let anyone become zealously active in bringing others to faith in Christ and — in some quarters at least — resentment and opposition are quick to develop. "In the world we have tribulation."

And the world has so many ways of getting at us, doesn't it? In some ages and places, persecution is the preferred strategy. Threats, ostracism, imprisonment, even martyrdom, may come to God's loyal servants. It may prove a painful and costly business to follow the Crucified. Some who are reading this right now may know how true that is. But the world has other methods of turning us away from God, other tactics to divert us from discipleship. If we can be led in subtle ways to adopt the values and outlook of the world, persecution may not even be needed.

And how vulnerable we are to those temptations! How easy it is to slip into self-indulgence instead of self-discipline, to value things more than people, to be more concerned about prestige than about integrity. Many of us want to live as Christians, want to be the Lord's servants, but find ourselves easily turned aside, either by the frowns or the smiles of this world.

But Christ's triumph gives us hope. Unlike most of history's leaders, Jesus does not conquer for Himself alone. His is not a triumph of personal ambition, an "ego trip" as we say. His victory was won for His people. He accomplished it, but they share it. Though they have tribulation in this world, in Him they have peace. He is soon to ascend to the Father, He says, and will send His Spirit to live in their hearts. They will still be joined to Him by invisible bonds as branches in the true vine. His life, His strength, His victory will be communicated to them. Though in themselves they are wayward and weak, He will enable them to remain faithful. "Whatever is born of God," says John, "overcomes the world." And this is the victory that overcomes the world, our faith. "Who is it that overcomes the world," asks the apostle, "but he who believes that Jesus is the Son of God." To trust in Him, crucified and risen for us as our one Savior and Lord, this makes His victory ours. We don't have to be intimidated or duped by this world. We don't need to be conformed to its pattern, squeezed into its mold. We can be God's people, loving Him first and best, doing His will here and now, seeking His kingdom.

But remember, it is only because we are united to Him, empowered by His Spirit. I heard recently that a minister had told his flock that Jesus no longer has the power of God to save, to heal, and to transform. According to this zealous brother, the Lord has passed on this power to His followers. They have it now. Perhaps the preacher wanted to assure his people that

God's power is really present in their lives, but the assurance came at the expense of truth. No one ever receives Christ's power and victory so as to become independent of Him. He remains the mighty Lord, accomplishing His purposes through His people. We can truthfully say, as believers, that we have overcome the world. But the only thing that keeps that claim from being ridiculous is the perfect victory of Christ in which we have come to share.

If you have never personally trusted in Jesus, He calls you today to follow Him, the Conqueror. He promises a hard road: "In the world you will have trouble." But "in me," He adds, "you can have peace." And more than that, when you belong to Him and rely on Him, the pressures of this age can never rob you of your true personhood, or steal your heart away from God. Rejoice in that. "Be of good cheer," He says; "I have overcome the world."

QUESTIONS FOR DISCUSSION

1. In what different senses is the word "world" used in the New Testament?

2. How did Jesus "overcome" the world?

3. In what ways have you especially felt the world's opposition?

4. How can we share in Christ's victory over the world?

24. What Is Eternal Life?

When Jesus had spoken these words, he lifted up his eyes to heaven and said, "Father, the hour has come; glorify thy Son that the Son may glorify thee, since thou hast given him power over all flesh, to give eternal life to all whom thou hast given him. And this is eternal life, that they know thee the only true God, and Jesus Christ whom thou hast sent."

(John 17:1-3)

EVERY NOW AND then, the local papers in Michigan carry pictures of those who have won fortunes in the state lottery. Sometimes we see them just after they have heard the news. As you might expect, there are big smiles, warm embraces, victory signs. Suppose now for a moment that someone came to those same people with authoritative news that they had been given eternal life. How would they react? According to Jesus, this is the treasure of lasting value, the supreme good. The whole purpose of God's love and Christ's coming was that people may have it. Without eternal life, He says, all of us are doomed to perish. With it, we find unspeakable joy. If there is such a thing, if the staggering promise is true, it is surely worth knowing about. What does eternal life really mean?

Listen to these words taken from a prayer which

Jesus prayed in the presence of His disciples on the night before He died: "And this is eternal life, that they know thee the only true God, and Jesus Christ whom thou hast sent." From this passage and from others like it in the gospels, we can say at least this much about Jesus' view of eternal life: first, it means *living,* not merely existing; second, it is *present* and not only future; and third, it is *knowing God* Himself and not simply enjoying ourselves.

Think with me about that first idea. Eternal life is a quality of living — not merely continued existence. All of us are familiar with the difference between barely eking out an existence and living a full life. Sometimes we speak of people living "at a subsistence level." They have just enough to keep body and soul together, just enough to remain in the land of the living, but not enough to do much living while they're here. Our slang expressions and exclamations often express the same idea: "This is the life!"; "Man, that's livin'!" We're talking then about a quality or intensity of life beyond the ordinary. The New Testament expresses that distinction by using two different words for life. One is the word *bios,* which means physical vitality, animal existence. In fact, it is the word from which we get the term *biology.* The other word, *zoe,* means life with a special quality about it. It is the term Jesus always uses when He talks about eternal life.

Everyone is concerned, of course, about finding "the good life." Politicians promise it to all; educators claim to be preparing the young for it; and the gifted, wealthy, cultured, influential people around us seem to have it. But, strangely, many of these favored people are not really happy with the life they have found. You know how that works. You think that life will really be complete if you can just reach the top in your profession, but when you get there it doesn't seem so great after all. Or, if you could only be comfortable financially, then life would take on a new brightness and freedom. But it doesn't always happen that way. Sometimes the most attractive, creative, successful people find life hardly worth the living.

When we realize this, it is small comfort to hear that scientists may soon be able to extend the length of human life, perhaps some day even providing immortality here in this world. By steadily lengthening our life expectancy until they finally find the means to prevent its ending, surgery and medicine will supposedly do away with death altogether. We will be like those ancient cars seen in auto shows, kept on the road indefinitely by replacing the worn-out parts. Instead of spark plugs and mufflers we will get new hearts, new lungs, new kidneys, even new brains, when and as we require them.

In the Bible, eternal life is a far cry from that. It doesn't mean grimly hanging on to life in this world or the bare survival of the human race, or even our continuing influence in future generations. It is a brand new life — a life which none of us inherit by nature, one that cannot be learned from books or bought with money. It is God's own kind of life, the life of the age to come.

That brings us to our second thought about eternal life. It is not only future, but also *present*. It is, of course, a future reality. The word *eternal* means, in the Greek language, "of or pertaining to an age." Eternal life is the life of an age or eon. In the New Testament that age is the coming one, the future beyond history, the prospect which God has prepared. Eternal life is the kind of life that will be lived then, the quality of life characteristic of God's future, when His purpose has been finally accomplished and His kingdom has fully come.

How good it is to know that there is life in the future! Here in this world everything — transplants notwithstanding — ends in death. And it is the dread that nothing, or at least nothing good, lies beyond death that robs this present life of meaning for many people. Face it squarely: what ends in nothing doesn't amount to very much. If death is a blank, an exit to nowhere, all talk about the good life is whistling in the dark, a buffer against despair. But the glad message of the Christian Gospel is that there *is* a life beyond. There is a coming age, and though the earth may burn or the sun may cool, there is a future for the children of men.

But to say that eternal life is future is to tell only half the story. The New Testament rings with the confidence that this life of the coming age has already broken into human history. Eternal life is not only *then,* it is also now. People can not only look forward to it, they can presently experience and enjoy it. How vital it is to see that! Christians have often been accused of using the future hope as an escape from the present. Marx called it "the opiate of the people," the drug by which the ruling classes keep the oppressed ones content with their lot. And whenever the Christian faith is set forth as offering rewards and blessings that are only future, its meaning is distorted. Sometimes Christians quote the words, "Eye hath not seen, nor ear heard, nor have entered into the heart of man, the things which God hath prepared for them that love him." That verse speaks of the future hope. But how often have you heard quoted the words which immediately follow: "But God hath revealed them unto us by his Spirit" (1 Cor. 2:9, 10, KJV). Eternal life is a new life beyond our power to grasp or appreciate, but by the power of the Holy Spirit we can even now begin to live it. The Holy Spirit is the Spirit of the coming age. He brings eternal life into our experience, giving us a glimpse of the glory, a foretaste of the heavenly feast, a first installment, as it were, of true life. That's why the New Testament speaks so much about people having eternal life right now.

But we haven't yet come to the heart of what it *means.* Hear this word of Jesus again: "This is eternal life, that they know thee the only true God, and Jesus Christ whom thou hast sent." Eternal life means knowing God Himself and not merely enjoying ourselves.

172

I'm afraid that latter idea about it is the most common with the average person — that heaven, eternal life, is a state of unalloyed bliss where we may enjoy ourselves to the full. For one group it may be a place of sensual pleasure, for another a happy hunting ground. And how many people have you heard say, only half in jest, that if heaven has no golf course or no fishing or shopping, they are not interested!

All such thinking about the life to come betrays a deep misunderstanding. It seems to imply that people can be perfectly blessed, genuinely fulfilled as human beings, without God being in the picture at all. But the whole message of the Bible speaks otherwise. At the beginning, the glory of man's creation was that he was made in God's image, for fellowship with Him. The deep tragedy of our sin was that we cut ourselves off from God, and in doing so turned away from each other. All the record of God's self-revealing, of His unfolding purpose in history, is the story of barriers broken down, of fellowship restored, of prodigals returning to the Father's house. It is for this that Christ became a man, lived among us and died in our place, that He might bring us to God. And in the visions of the Book of Revelation, the crowning blessedness of heaven is expressed in words like these: "Behold, the dwelling of God is with men. He will dwell with them, and they shall be his people, and God himself will be with them; he will wipe away every tear from their eyes, and death shall be no more, neither shall there be mourning nor crying nor pain any more, for the former things have passed away" (Rev. 21: 3, 4). Here, where God's people are freed from all sorrows and evils, their highest joy is this: that God Himself will be with them and they will see His face.

That's what Jesus is expressing when He says that life eternal is to know the only true God — not merely to know about Him, but to know Him in personal relationship. Eternal life is not some blessing for which knowing God prepares us or qualifies us. This

173

knowing of Him is itself the life. Have we really grasped that? Have we stopped imagining that the gifts can somehow be more valuable than the Giver? Have we begun to understand, in the familiar words of a historic creed that "man's chief end is to glorify God and to enjoy him forever"? Eternal life is life from God, with God, in God. That's why there can be no heaven for those who want to shut God out of their lives, for those who have no time for Him and no inclination to worship Him. They would be miserable in heaven, for there God is all in all. They would have no taste for it, no capacity for enjoying eternal life; for that means knowing God, dwelling in His presence, adoring Him, and rejoicing in Him forever. It isn't that eternal life means merely sitting around through endless ages, strumming a harp and singing hymns. Jesus seems to hint in His parables that there are higher responsibilities there, a further trust to fulfill. But at the heart of everything is an entrance into the joy of one's Lord, living with Him, celebrating His love. And this knowledge of God which is eternal life can begin right now.

How then can we have it? How can we come to a living knowledge of God? The word of the Gospel tells us that knowing God is bound up with knowing Jesus Christ, whom God has sent. How can we find the invisible God? As He has made Himself visible in the incarnate life of Jesus, His Son. How can we hear God's voice? In listening to the words of Him who came to bring the Father's message. In Christ, God comes to us, calling us, inviting us. In Christ He comes near to us, holds out His hand to us, allows us to approach Him and know Him. When you believe in Jesus Christ, you are putting your trust in the living God who made heaven and earth and who gave His Son on your behalf. When you know Christ you have begun to know the only true God. Receiving Christ in faith, you receive the life that is life indeed. Here is the whole story of the Bible, the greatest love story ever told. "For God so loved the world that he gave his only begotten Son, that whoever believes in him should not perish but have eternal life."

Believe now in the love of God for you, in the gift of His Son on your behalf. Welcome Jesus Christ into your life in faith; and as you do, you can know with deep assurance that eternal life is yours now and will always be. Then you will be truly rich, and ready to live for His praise and enjoy Him forever!

QUESTIONS FOR DISCUSSION

1. What does the lately popular phrase "quality of life" mean to you?

2. How would you distinguish "real life" from mere survival?

3. What special significance does the word "eternal" have for an understanding of the life we find in Christ?

4. What inadequate views of God and of the life to come are exposed and corrected by this passage?

25. The King Nobody Wanted

Upon this Pilate sought to release him, but the Jews cried out, "If you release this man, you are not Caesar's friend; every one who makes himself a king sets himself against Caesar." When Pilate heard these words, he brought Jesus out and sat down on the judgment seat at a place called The Pavement, and in Hebrew, Gabbatha. Now it was the day of Preparation of the Passover; it was about the sixth hour. He said to the Jews, "Behold your King!" They cried out, "Away with him, away with him, crucify him!" Pilate said to them, "Shall I crucify your King?" The chief priests answered, "We have no king but Caesar."

(John 19:12-15)

IT'S A DANGEROUS thing, they say, to mix religion with politics. At a governors' conference some time ago, one of our state leaders was warned that if he continued to take a certain stand on the basis of his religious convictions, he would be committing political suicide. On the other side of it, preachers are sometimes cautioned not to become too involved in politics. More than one minister has found that when he introduced contemporary issues into his pulpit proclamation, the mixture proved to be explosive. "Danger — Do Not Touch!" That's the warning often addressed to a religious man when he becomes active politically.

No one ever exposed himself to that peril more radically than did Jesus Christ. He was a religious teacher par excellence. He spoke as from God and proclaimed the way to God. He was dealing continually with the most profound religious questions. But that was not all. He also made claims about Himself — claims with far-reaching political implications. In fact, He made the supreme political claim; He said He was a king. And that was a very dangerous thing to say. Around that issue raged a whirlwind of controversy which finally swept Him to His death.

The gospel writers, especially John, go out of their way to show us how prominent this matter of kingship was in the events that led up to Jesus' crucifixion. Was He a king or not? That issue was always at the eye of the storm. When He entered Jerusalem on a donkey, the excited crowds ran to meet Him with palm branches in their hands, crying, "Hosanna! Blessed is he who comes in the name of the Lord, even the King of Israel" (John 12:13). Many of the religious leaders were offended and disturbed at this. They said to one another, "You see that you can do nothing. Look, the world has gone after Him." They determined then that something had to be done about it.

When Jesus later stood on trial before the Roman governor, Pilate's first question was, "Are you the King of the Jews?" Apparently this was the charge that had been passed along by the Jewish court. After Jesus' response, Pilate pursued the question further: "So you *are* a king." That possibility continued to haunt him. When he offered the crowd the release of one prisoner, Pilate said, "Will you have me release for you the King of the Jews?" This seemed only to excite their rage. They cried out again, "Not this man, but Barabbas!"

The question of whether or not Jesus was king had become common talk all over Jerusalem. The soldiers to whom Jesus was delivered for scourging were highly amused by it. One of them hit on the idea of making a mock crown of thorns and of robing the prisoner in royal purple. Then they lined up to render their obeisance to the "king." It wasn't often that they could slap royalty full in the face!

When Pilate later brought Jesus out to the crowd again, no one missed the symbolism of the robe and thorny diadem. The cries of hatred were more intense: "Crucify him! Crucify him!" Pilate, knowing Jesus' innocence, wanted to release Him; but again it was the kingly claim which stood in the way. Jesus' enemies knew how to apply political pressure. "If you release this man," they cried, "you are not Caesar's friend; every one who makes himself a king sets himself against Caesar." That settled it for Pilate. This was too nasty a case to dismiss. For one last time he brought his prisoner before the crowd, taunting them, "Behold your King!" When they screamed again for blood, Pilate angered them still further. "Shall I crucify your king?" he asked.

And that wasn't all. Pilate carried the idea of royalty even further. If the Jews were going to force him into this execution, then he would have his fun at their expense. Pilate had a title written in three languages and affixed to Jesus' cross: "Jesus of Nazareth, the King of the Jews." The chief priests were furious. "Don't write, 'The King of the Jews,' " they protested, "but, 'This man said "I am the King of the Jews." ' " But Pilate was adamant now. "What I have written, I have written."

We wonder why this issue was so tense, so charged with murderous feeling. But isn't the question of sovereignty, of rule, always that way? The reason lies in the challenge offered to existing powers by a new ruler. Claimants to a throne never arise in a vacuum. Rather, they collide with the existing order. They challenge the powers that be. How could there be room for another king in Caesar's Rome? There could be puppets, yes, vassals to the emperor, but no one with kingly rights, no one with the power of life and death. Caesar tolerated no rivals. Even to acknowledge that there might

178

be another king could get any Roman official in deep trouble.

And Israel, too, even though a subject people, had its own hierarchy, its own establishment. There was a religious authority to be exercised, a control over the minds and spirits of men, about which Israel's leaders were jealous. Any new political figure jeopardized that regime. And the more popular he was with the masses, the more dangerous he was to have around.

But there is a deeper, more personal level at which new kings meet with opposition. In each human heart, slave or free, ruled or ruler, there is a central throne on which sits "King Self." This is the rule we cherish most dearly, the sovereignty we struggle hardest to protect. We want to run our own lives. We want to go our own way. We insist on our "crown rights." Woe to the man who presumes to take them from us! And if Jesus Christ really is the king He claims to be, then every empire, great or small, is directly challenged.

But is He a king after all? To Pilate the whole idea seemed ludicrous. In his first words to Jesus, "Are you the King of the Jews?" the emphasis falls, in the original language, on the word "you." In other words, it was a kind of incredulous question. "*You? Are you* the King of the Jews?" At the very least, a king wields power and has subjects under his sway. But Pilate was dealing here with a harmless peasant, at the mercy of both the Jewish and Roman courts, with no one to plead His case, much less to fight in His defense. This character a king? Where are His crown and scepter? Where His castle and His throne? What nation does He rule? What land can He call His own? Where are the legions which He can command? The claim seemed so far-fetched that Pilate had a hard time taking it seriously. To the soldiers, too, Jesus' seeming defenselessness made a joke out of any pretentions to a throne. To lift a hand against a real king would be flirting with death, they well knew; but they could slap this prisoner around as they pleased.

To the leaders of Jesus' own nation, however, His kingly claims were no joke. They had seen something of His power to sway men. They had grasped clearly what His claim meant. To them it was sheer blasphemy. God Himself—the God of Abraham, Isaac, and Jacob — was Israel's true king. But here was a man who claimed that the kingly rule of God Himself had arrived in His person. Who could stand for that — a man insisting that He was the king of heaven come to earth?

So there it was — the kingship of Jesus: to the Romans, a laughing stock; to the Jews, a sacrilege. But to John the apostle, and many others like him, it was the truth. Yes, the *gospel* truth. John, of course, was writing in the light of Easter morning, from the perspective of an empty tomb. He wrote as one whose eyes had seen the risen Lord, whose life had been transformed by meeting Him. The heart of the message these Christians brought to the world was simply this: Jesus is Lord, Christ is king.

Is that such a joke, Pilate? You laughed at His weakness but His rule has shaped the world more than did a thousand of your Caesars. Today, people by the tens of millions march at Christ's command. You priests and scribes, was it really blasphemous for Him to claim what He did? What if God really did come to us in Him? What if we crucified our king?

He's another kind of king, of course. Hardly the type to which we are accustomed. His kingdom, as He told Pilate, is not of this world. It was not gained by force of arms. Nor is it furthered by the weapons and methods of this age. His is a kingdom of truth, which only seekers after truth will ever recognize. His dominion does not enslave men but liberates them. This king rules only that He may make kings of all His subjects. Further, Christ has founded His kingdom in lowly, suffering love. Eyes of faith can see His sufferings now in the splendor of a new light. That apparent weakness was power in disguise. Behind men's murderous cry, "Crucify him!" was God's "Long live the

King!" The cross which seemed to mock His kingship turned out to be His royal throne. Christ *rules* from that cross. The power by which He subdues men's hearts to Himself is that poured-out love, that self-giving all the way to death for the sin of the world. One of history's mightiest rulers, Napoleon, marveled at such power. Listen to his words: "Alexander, Caesar, Charlemagne, and myself founded empires. But on what did we rest the creations of our genius? Upon force. Jesus Christ alone founded his empire upon love, and at this hour millions of men would die for him." Think about it. Who else ever ruled so many and was served so freely?

Christ's kingdom, though it is not *of* this world, is certainly *in* this world. His kingship makes a difference in the common stuff of history. It may be dangerous to mix religion with politics, but there is no way to avoid it if Jesus Christ is king. His rule touches every aspect of life. It claims all of a man, in all his relationships and activities. That's why those who proclaim His rule are often seen as a threat. The early Christians were accused of "acting against the decrees of Caesar, saying that there is another king, Jesus." The fiery preacher, Savonarola, cried aloud in Florence, Italy, almost five hundred years ago, "It is the Lord's will to give a new head to this city of Florence. The new head is Christ. Christ seeks to become your king!" Hearts made strong by that conviction are always the foes of tyranny, of absolute political power. Even in a democracy like ours, to stand for Christ's kingdom may arouse opposition. Christians insist that what the nation does is not right just because the nation does it. They serve a Lord whose will stands above every party platform and to whom all who govern will finally give account.

There are still some who, like Pilate, laugh this off as ridiculous. Many others still say of Christ, "We will not have this man to reign over us." But the kingship of Jesus, whatever people think of it, is not a pious phrase but a fact. God has raised Him from the dead and given Him dominion. God has made Him both Lord and Christ and pledged that the day will come when every knee will bow to Him and every tongue acknowledge His lordship.

It was one of the most tragic moments of history when those who claimed to be God's people said, "We have no king but Caesar." It is still tragic when men today own no higher authority than national power or narrow self-interest. If Jesus Christ is king, then He is the only One with a total claim on our lives, the only One to whom ultimate allegiance belongs. He wins it from us, not by force of arms, but by His truth and by the conquering power of His love. To believe in Him is to render total, willing submission. Have you done that? Will you? He is a king worth serving. "Bring forth the royal diadem and crown Him Lord of all."

QUESTIONS FOR DISCUSSION

1. What do people mean when they say that "religion should not be mixed with politics"? What truth do you see in this statement? What falsehood?

2. How were the Jews and the Romans affected differently by Jesus' claim to be King?

3. What inner resistance do all of us raise against acknowledging a *king*?

4. If Christ's kingdom is not "of this world," what difference does it make in human history?

26. Accomplished!

After this Jesus, knowing that all was now finished, said (to fulfill the scripture), "I thirst." A bowl of vinegar stood there; so they put a sponge full of the vinegar on hyssop and held it to his mouth. When Jesus had received the vinegar, he said, "It is finished"; and he bowed his head and gave up his spirit.

(John 19:28-30)

"LAST WORDS" HAVE an awesome quality about them. The final speeches of dying loved ones are apt to linger long in our memories. We listen for such expressions with eagerness. We strain forward to hear them. We savor their meaning and call them to mind long afterward. We like to repeat them to each other. Those last words seem to gather up and express so much about the one who spoke them — what his life was like, the contribution that it made, the effects it continues to have on others. And the closer we are to these persons, the more deeply we are affected by the last things they say.

Christians often dwell on the words which Jesus spoke from the cross in the last hours of His suffering. How much about Him is crystalized in those brief sentences! Some were spoken to individuals around

His cross, some were breathed toward God in prayer. But there was one word that He seemed to want everyone around Him to hear. Two of the gospel writers, Matthew and Mark, tell us that Jesus cried out with a loud voice just before He died. It is John who tells us just what that cry was.

As Jesus knew that His sufferings were about to end, He said, "I thirst." Earlier He had refused the potion of drugged wine that would have eased His pain. He had wanted to face those sufferings with a clear mind. But now death was very near and there was a final word He wanted to speak. Perhaps He craved a drink, something to clear His throat, so that He could speak clearly. At any rate, when the sponge full of vinegar had touched His mouth, He cried out, "It is finished." Then He dropped His head and breathed His last.

As we try to place ourselves at that scene and listen to those words, what do we hear? For one thing, we catch a strange note of *victory*. Jesus' last word is not a sigh but a shout. He seems to be exulting rather than complaining. He sounds more like a conqueror than a victim.

You can notice this paradox all the way through the final events of Jesus' life. A large company of men, heavily armed, comes out to arrest Him, carrying lanterns and torches so that their suspect will not be able to escape into the darkness. But when they arrive in the garden, Jesus steps boldly forward, startling the leaders of the expedition so greatly that they slump backward to the ground. Even though they arrest and bind Him, He somehow seems to be in charge of what is happening. He is quiet before the high priest and the hired accusers, yet they seem more to be on trial than He. Pilate assumes that he has Jesus' destiny in his hands, but as they talk we gain the impression that it's the other way around. By the majesty of His presence, Jesus makes even the words spoken of Him in contempt to gain the ring of truth. "Behold the man!" "Behold your king!" "He saved others." "Jesus of

184

Nazareth, the King of the Jews." And now when He comes to die, though rejected, humiliated, and twisted with pain, He ends His life with a triumphant shout.

When we see someone face death that way, it makes us shake our heads in wonder. Some cower and cringe before death's approach. Others face it stoically, with calm resignation. And both of these we can understand. But when people die in a way that seems to challenge and defy death itself, we marvel. They seem so sure of what's happening to them. They seem to know something that others do not grasp.

As Dwight L. Moody was growing older, he once spoke to a group of people about his own death. "One of these days," he said, "you'll read in the paper that Dwight L. Moody is dead. Don't you believe it. I'll be more alive than I've ever been before!" There it is again — that note of triumph.

When my own mother was lying in a New York hospital, desperately ill with cancer, I was given the difficult task of breaking the news to her. As we talked, I found (as so often happens) that she already knew. For several moments we talked quietly about what was ahead. Then she told me about something that had happened the night before in her hospital room. The lights of the city, shining in through the window, had etched a giant "V" on the wall opposite her bed. As she lay there, half thinking, half praying, the gleaming shape on the wall became for her a kind of sign. "I knew then," she said, "that whatever happened, it was going to be *victory*." I wonder, will it be that way for me, for you? Will there be a hint of trumpets and something of sunrise in the moment of death for us? Will it be in any sense a time to shout and sing?

But we hear more in that last outcry of Jesus. There is also a note of *accomplishment* about His life. That's what the word "It is finished" actually mean. Not so much, "It's all over," as "It's completely done." His ambitions were realized. The work of His life was fulfilled. That's what He meant.

185

Christ was mastered throughout His whole career by a sense of divine destiny. At His every step He was conscious of God's command. He always did those things that pleased the Father. And even when He hung helpless on a cross He knew that He was accomplishing something — the very thing that He came to do.

The meaning of our death is all bound up with the kind of life that has gone before it. It's possible to look at life simply as something that happens to you. You drift along through it, hoping for a few lucky breaks, avoiding as many troubles as you can. And then you die as you live. Your life comes to an end. It trails away into nothing. You finally give in to what you can't avoid.

But there is another way of living — a way shot through with purpose. You're in this world *for* something. You have a race to run, a battle to fight, a work to do. And you're immortal until the work is done. That makes death seem different, doesn't it?

From one standpoint, Jesus' dying seems tragic. He was a man in the prime of life, with so much to live for and so much to give to the world. Here He was — cut off in a brutal, senseless execution. And yet He cries, "It is finished." Mission accomplished! All that He came for had been determined, dared, and done.

That underlies for us the fact that a life is not measured by its length in years or by its apparent success. Christ filled His life full with obedience. He was faithful all the way to death. And so when He came to die, it was only the last step of a road He had chosen to walk. When He bowed His head and gave up His spirit it was as though He died by choice and not by force. It was an achievement rather than an accident. He had really lived.

The same "filling-up" of life appears in many of Christ's followers. The Apostle Paul, for example, was absorbed by the thought that God had appointed certain tasks for him. Nothing moved him from completing those tasks. Finishing his course with joy, fulfilling the ministry given to him meant more to Paul than personal safety — more than life itself. How this gives dignity, meaning, and grandeur to human life, when our meat and drink is to do the Father's will! When this is the great aim for which we live, then death can never rob life of meaning. Whenever and however it ends, the life surrendered to God has a kind of completeness about it.

Without that, life never seems long enough. Whatever its duration, it lacks what will really last. Without a link to God's great design in our lives, we can all identify with poor Willy Loman in Miller's *Death of a Salesman*. He said, "I still feel — kind of temporary about myself." Is your life like that now: temporary, tentative, unfulfilled? What crowning significance will death have when it comes for you?

I hear one more message in that final shout of the Savior from the cross — a note of *assurance* for us. The words "It is finished" actually translate a single Greek word, *tetelesthai*. That verb is in the perfect tense, which in the Greek language has a special significance. It stands for an action in the past which has continuing effects in the present. That means, in other words, that the work which Christ accomplished then still has significance for us today. His death, though it happened long ago, is not simply a remote fact of ancient history. The power released in it is still at work — now!

What Christ accomplished on the cross, in obedience to the Father's will, was done for us. The old hymn expresses it simply and well: "He died that we might be forgiven, He died to make us good, That we might go at last to heaven, Saved by His precious blood." It was a saving, redeeming work that He did on our behalf. And His cry, "It is finished," assures us that His deed is sufficient. Its effects continue now and forever. Nothing can or need be added to it. In His obedience unto death our salvation was accomplished.

What does that mean for us now? It means that everything necessary for us to be forgiven and accepted by the Holy One, everything needed to bring us into a right relationship with God has already taken place. There is absolutely nothing we can do to enhance our standing with God or make ourselves more acceptable in His sight. That great work has been done, done perfectly and done forever. We can contribute nothing to what He did there; we can only receive it with a believing heart.

Imagine that a priceless Rembrandt hangs before you. You stand there drinking in its beauty, marveling at the consummate artistry that produced it. Would you consider picking up a brush to add a few strokes of your own? Of course not! It's a finished work. And so it is with the infinitely greater work of Jesus Christ for the redemption of the world. It would be presumption to try to add to it. It is ours to behold, to appreciate, to respond to.

Here is why Christian faith rings and sings with assurance — because it rests entirely on the perfect work of Christ. If our hope for eternal life depended in any part on our efforts, we could never be sure of it, could we? We would never know that we had done enough or that what we had done would make the grade. But if our destiny depends one hundred percent on the one sacrifice which Christ offered on the cross, then we can be sure about it. His work will not be found wanting. Grounded on that, I can be free from forebodings about the future, free to live gratefully here and now.

O friend, has it dawned on you that Christ's work on your behalf has been perfectly accomplished? Think of it this way. God declares in His Word that what Christ has done for you is fully sufficient. You believe in your heart of hearts that He did it for you, and on that basis you can be joyfully, humbly secure. God said it, Christ did it, you believe it, and that settles it.

Listen again to this great word of Jesus Christ: "It

is finished." Hear the note of victory in the face of death, of accomplishment in life, of assurance for all who trust Him. Listen with all your heart to that triumphant shout. His last words are meant for you.

QUESTIONS FOR DISCUSSION

1. Why do a person's "last words" seem so significant to us?

2. How would you describe the Christian attitude toward death? Denial? Delight? Defiance?

3. How was Christ's dying expressive of the way He lived His entire life?

4. What ground of assurance do we have in the fact that Christ's saving work is "finished"?

27. Easter Gifts

On the evening of that day, the first day of the week,
the doors being shut where the disciples were, for fear
of the Jews, Jesus came and stood among them and
said to them, "Peace be with you." When he had said
this, he showed them his hands and his side. Then the
disciples were glad when they saw the Lord. Jesus said
to them again, "Peace be with you. As the Father has
sent me, even so I send you." And when he had said
this, he breathed on them, and said to them, "Receive
the Holy Spirit."

(John 20:19-22)

EASTER WAS THE day when I began to live again. Up
until that morning, life had seemed to be ebbing away.
I was a sick seven-year-old. A victim of ear trouble
almost from the day I was born, I had struggled through
each winter with a series of ear infections. Each one
seemed to get worse. One cold day in February, I was
taken into the hospital for an emergency mastoid opera-
tion. The surgery was quite extensive. When that was
all over, it was found that I had contracted erysipelas,
a blood ailment, and had to be transferred to a hospital
for contagious diseases. After that, things seemed to
go downhill fast. One blood test followed another, with
every imaginable form of treatment, but nothing helped.

By Good Friday, the doctors wondered if I would make it. A blood transfusion was scheduled for Sunday morning as a kind of last resort. My father was to be the donor. He gave me his blood in a direct transfusion, arm to arm. On that morning, Easter, a faintly flickering young life was kindled again, and I was on my way to health.

That was many years ago, but I can still recall the scene so clearly. They brought me, frightened and whimpering, into a special room. But there was my dad, lying on a bed beside mine, and I soon quieted down. The whole experience gave me a special closeness to him, a deep appreciation for what he had done. He gave part of his life to me, so that I could live. That was my dad's Easter gift.

It wasn't until years later, though, that I began to grasp what Easter means for all of us. Now faith lights up my childhood experience with fresh meaning. I see it as a vivid picture of what God did on that first Easter. That was the day when a dying world began to live again.

Try to picture the scene. It is the first day of the week, at evening. You are inside a locked room somewhere in Jerusalem. Several men are sitting around a low table, talking with subdued excitement about the rumors they have heard. Two are pacing the room with quick, nervous steps. One big fellow sits by himself, head cupped in his hands; for once Simon Peter has nothing to say. Suddenly another figure stands before them. Conversation dies in a gasp. Next, a stunned silence. Then His word: "Peace." Still no one moves. He lifts His hands and turns slightly so that each can see. Nail prints. And, lest any doubt should linger, there — under His heart — He points to the mark of the spear. It was He — Jesus their Lord; and His word to them was *shalom:* "Peace be to you." There was His Easter gift.

And how they needed it! The crucifixion had left them crushed and desolate. Their hopes and dreams had seemed to die with Him on Good Friday. Now they were saddened by their loss, confused and anxious, afraid of those who had condemned their Master. They were like many today whose hopes have been disappointed, whose loved ones have been taken from them, who are anxious and restless about what is happening in the world. Some have called ours the Atomic Age or the Space Age, but perhaps the Aspirin Age would be more appropriate. Our world knows little real peace. But there stands Christ on Easter Sunday, speaking peace to those first followers, and to us.

What were the ingredients of that peace? What did it mean to those who first heard it and received it? There was the banishing of doubt in the assurance that Christ was all that He had claimed to be. Their faith in Him had been terribly tested in those last hours. So much had happened that seemed to mock His claim. He was dead, and all hope had semed to die with Him. Was He really the one the world had been waiting for? It was hard to believe that when evil had seemed to swallow Him up. But now there He was — alive — and they knew now that He was the Lord. Peace meant also the conquest of fear. Evil had seemed invincible during the hours of His sufferings. His enemies seemed to be in control of everything. Death had proved too much even for their Master. Now what was to become of them? But when He stood there, speaking His word of peace, it meant that death and hell had been conquered and there was nothing to be afraid of any more. And with that peace, that triumphant confidence, came joy. "The disciples were glad when they saw the Lord." It meant the end of sadness. The One they loved most was not gone after all. He was with them still. Everything seemed different to them now. They felt good about life again. That was His gift of peace.

But Christ had more to bestow than that. Along with His peace came the gift of *purpose*. "As the Father has sent me," He said, "even so I send you." A few days earlier life for the disciples had been suddenly robbed of meaning. Christ's call had made them what they were. What was left to live for after He was gone? That loss of meaning has devastating effects upon people. The noted psychotherapist Victor Frankl sees the will to find meaning as the most significant quest in human life. In fact, he claims that patients with mental disorders can only be aided toward recovery "if we can manage to give them some content for their lives, if we can help them find an aim and a purpose in their existence." How many that you and I know today seem frustrated because their life and work are meaningless!

Imagine that you and your fellow workers are ordered to dig a hole in the courtyard of your plant. You toil and sweat, digging the hole. Then your superior comes over, looks in it, and tells you to fill it back up. Next you're commanded to dig another hole in a different place. You dig again and the same thing happens. After that has been repeated a few more times you and your fellow workers are angry enough to fight — or quit. It's only when your boss explains that he's looking for a break in an underground piping system that you can begin to calm down. If the task has meaning, if we can see some purpose in our toil, it's bearable.

Jesus Christ gives life new meaning for multitudes of His followers in His word of commissioning: "As the Father has sent me, even so I send you." He was sent to bear witness to the truth, and so are we. In a world of the big lie and the half-truth, we are to be the heralds of a message from God that makes sense of things, enabling men to "see life steadily and see it whole." He was sent to seek and to save that which was lost; and so are we to have the shepherd heart, seeking for wanderers. He came not to be served but to serve. That outlines our task, too — to be a servant people, ministering in love to the needs of those around us. We, like our Savior, are sent ones on a mission in this world. We are linked with God's purpose, sharing in the most significant work that human beings were ever given to do. To be gripped by that sense of divine destiny, to be commissioned by a Lord like that, to a work like His — what more could anyone ask?

But there *is* more — more that Christ gives to His people. Along with His peace and a new sense of purpose, He gave them *power*. Whenever we're confronted with a great calling, we feel keenly our own shortcomings. Remember Moses? Even a great revelation and a deep sense of calling were not enough to dispel his anxieties about himself. "Who am I," he asks, "that I should go to Pharaoh?" And many of the disciples, perhaps, felt the same. They knew they had already failed their Lord badly, and they wondered if they could really trust anything about themselves any more. They were commissioned to a tremendous work, but were they sufficient for it?

We also struggle with fears about ourselves. Perhaps you were never able to express yourself in the family circle as a child. You wonder, "Will I ever be able to communicate the good news to others?" Or you feel that your educational background limits you. Perhaps you don't feel at ease with people. More than that, you know how dismally you've failed before. You wince at the treacheries of your own heart. You suffer under the accusing voice that whispers, "You're not much of a Christian yourself. Who are you to share this with someone else?" But upon all of us, beset with fears, filled with self-doubt, as on those men in that locked room, Christ breathes and says, "Receive the Holy Spirit."

Do we grasp what is happening here? Note the promise of Jesus in the last words of Matthew's gospel: "Lo, I am with you all the days." Read also in the second chapter of Acts about the coming of the Spirit on the day of Pentecost. Then see how here in John's gospel is revealed the link between the two. It is Jesus Christ, the risen Lord, who sends the Spirit on Pentecost. And the Spirit He sends is the gift of His own in-breathed life! This equips them, this makes them adequate for whatever He may summon them to do. It's not simply that He says, "Here, you go out in My service and I'll help you over the rough spots." No, it's, "Here, take My life; I give it to you. I *create* your ministry."

Isn't that what He meant in the very beginning? His call was, "Follow me and I will *make you* fishers of men." They had learned about that in a number of ways. Once they fished all night and took nothing; but when they put down their nets at His word, they could hardly haul in the catch of fish. Once they had only a snack of loaves and fish to feed a famished crowd. But when they put that little bit in His hands, He gave it back; and then there was more than enough. They began to glimpse the fact that the miracle work they were sent to do was really His doing. He was giving them their apostleship. He was breathing eternity into it. Whatever would count and grow and flourish and last would be His work, though they would be busy planting and watering. He would make it happen. And they who felt so helpless would be able to say, as Paul did, "I can do all things in him who strengthens me" (Phil. 4:13).

Those, then, are the bestowals of the risen Lord — His Easter gifts. In a real sense they resolve themselves into one: His own presence, His in-breathed life. Christ, the living One, is with His people! And that unspeakable gift calls for one great response — the faith that *receives*.

In a sense, what happened in that upper room was unique. They saw His wounds; they heard with their ears His voice of commissioning; they felt on their faces His quickening breath. It will not happen for us in just that way. But the glory of the Easter message is that it does happen! Christ still meets with His gathered people; He still speaks in the word of the Gospel, and the winds of His Spirit are still blowing. Oh, believe that! He speaks peace to you. He brings purpose to you. He breathes power into you. Open your heart wide in faith and prayer to welcome His gifts. "Receive," He says, "the Holy Spirit." And for you, too, life will spring up again on Easter. His risen life, inbreathed by the Spirit, will put new heart in you. And then, alive in Him, go out to live all your days in gratitude for His Easter gift.

QUESTIONS FOR DISCUSSION

1. What did Christ's "peace" convey to the disciples on that Easter evening? How does it affect your life now?

2. How is Christ's being sent by the Father the same as our being sent by Christ?

3. What is usually the biggest obstacle in the way of fulfilling a God-given task?

4. What insight and encouragement are provided by Christ's *breathing* on His disciples when He said, "Receive the Holy Spirit"?

28. Great Believing

*Now Thomas, one of the twelve, called the Twin, was
not with them when Jesus came. So the other disciples
told him, "We have seen the Lord." But he said to
them, "Unless I see in his hands the print of the
nails, and place my finger in the mark of the nails, and
place my hand in his side, I will not believe." Eight
days later, his disciples were again in the house, and
Thomas was with them. The doors were shut, but
Jesus came and stood among them, and said, "Peace
be with you." Then he said to Thomas, "Put your finger
here, and see my hands; and put out your hand, and
place it in my side; do not be faithless, but believing."
Thomas answered him, "My Lord and my God!"*

(John 20:24-28)

THEY CALL ME "Doubting Thomas." That, of course,
isn't my real name. The "doubting" part has a story
behind it. And the word "Thomas" actually means
twin — one of a pair. That's what I've always been
known as — the Twin.

I guess I've always felt like a twin, too. For as long
as I can remember, people have compared me to my
brother. Joseph was taller and stronger than I, though
we looked very much alike. He was cheerful, happy as
a bird in the springtime; but I've never found it easy to

rejoice. Everything seemed to go well for him, but my early life seemed to be one long series of disappointments — I never succeeded much in sports and games, in work, or in love. More important, my brother was a religious man, in the good sense. Not me, though. From my early teens I've been something of a skeptic.

That's why it was so hard to believe when Jesus called me. It was on a day when He was speaking to a big crowd down by the lake. I went mostly out of curiosity, like everyone else in Capernaum. It was something to hear Him speak — a strong voice, yet mellow and clear as a bell. That impressed me right from the start. But when I got closer it was His eyes. Though I was fairly near the front of the crowd, there were some tall fishermen in front of me partly blocking my view. Still, whenever I got a glimpse of His face, it seemed that He was looking right at me.

After He had finished speaking I asked a question or two. Some of my friends said later that I was baiting Him. Maybe I was. I wasn't too sure about Him at first. But when He answered me, I began to feel embarrassed. He was so *genuine*. I could tell He really wanted me to know the truth.

When the meeting was over I started to drift back home with the crowd. After I had gone a little ways, people around me suddenly stopped talking. Just then I felt a hand on my shoulder, and when I turned around, I saw those eyes again. "Are you the man they call the Twin?" He asked. When I admitted that I was, He said, "I'd like you to come with Me."

I was scared. I could feel my face get pale — and then red. "What have I done?" I stammered. Then He smiled and said, "Come on." As He walked back toward the shore, I found myself following Him. "What am I doing?" I wondered. "What does He want with me? What good would I be to Him? My brother, maybe; he's the type. But not me. Maybe He has me mixed up with someone else."

Well, that's how it started. It turned out that I was

the one He was after. Soon I left my job and traveled with Him all the time. There were twelve of us then. No one of us could explain just how we got together. It just happened. We were all different, but we all knew that He wanted us, and that somehow we had to be with Him.

It's hard to explain the effect He had on us. He made God seem real, and for me that was quite something! Believe me, I'm not the kind of man to be taken in easily. I watched Him carefully. I noticed how He felt about people and what He did for them. That moved me. And what a person He was to be around! He never pushed Himself on you and yet you wanted to be with Him. I never got tired of hearing Him talk, or watching Him deal with people. His open, kind, fearless way of living made me ashamed of myself, and yet He also made me feel like I was somebody special. A lot of what He taught I didn't always understand, but I grew to love Him like a brother — and more than a brother. He was far above me, and I knew that. But He was the best friend I ever had. I really think He cared more about me than He did about Himself.

It wasn't long before He became a controversial figure. Everywhere we went people were talking about Him. You wouldn't believe how bitter some of the religious leaders became. It made me sick to see the way they tried to knife Him in the back, twisting His words and turning the people against Him — all because He didn't fit in with their system and wouldn't go along with their petty rules. But they hardly dared to tangle with Him face to face. When they did He could stand them on their ears! They would think they had Him in a corner, and then He'd ask them a question that they couldn't handle. They'd stammer around or huddle up to find an answer. All the while the people around would be laughing at them.

As time went on, He got more and more popular and the authorities got more hostile. I began to feel uneasy about it. I could see that there was trouble ahead — bad trouble. His enemies meant business. They weren't going to stop at anything. One day in Judea they had the crowd on the verge of stoning Him. We barely got away in time. I knew then He'd be in real danger if He ever got near Jerusalem again.

A few days later, word came from Bethany that a friend of His, Lazarus, was sick. When Jesus heard that, He told us that we were going back, back to Judea. We reminded Him of what had just happened but that didn't seem to bother Him. He was determined to go. We all were upset, but none of us was about to let Him go there alone. If that was the way it had to be, we decided that we would go along too — and die with Him.

After that, things began to happen fast. I'll never forget the day when He called Lazarus out of the tomb or how we felt the day He rode into Jerusalem. The crowd was going wild, cheering and spreading palm branches in the road. People loved Him! They called Him "the King." But that made His enemies all the more determined to get rid of Him.

We all sensed that something big was about to happen. During those days He began to talk a lot about how He was going away. He acted as though we understood it all. I remember when we were together in that upper room, how He said, "You know where I'm going and you know the way." Well, I can't speak for the others, but I sure didn't understand, and I told Him so. "Lord, we don't know where You're going and how can we know the way?" He talked for a long while after that; but I was feeling so bad, so confused, that a lot of it just didn't sink in.

When we finally left that upper room it was fairly late and we headed for the garden outside the city where we often camped. We weren't there very long when we saw the torches of a big crowd coming toward us. We began to fear the worst. Soon we saw that they were soldiers. And *Judas,* of all people, was leading them! He was a traitor, after all. Sure enough, they had come there to arrest Jesus. You know, He didn't even try to get away. He turned Himself right over to them. We didn't know what to make of it. Most of us just slipped away into the shadows.

From then on it was like one long nightmare. I could weep every time I think about it. They called it a trial; they called it justice. But it was a frame-up from the start. He never had a chance. When Pilate got hold of the case he knew that Jesus was innocent and yet to save his own political skin he went along with their scheme. The soldiers mocked Jesus and beat Him. What hurt even worse was the way the crowds screamed for His death, when Pilate brought Him outside.

The next day they crucified Him and I watched it all from a hillside. That was the blackest day of my life. I couldn't believe it was really happening. Maybe God would still step in and save Him. But when they plunged that spear into His side, I knew it was the end.

I can't begin to tell you how I felt. After it was over I didn't want to see anyone. Sometimes when the bottom drops out in life, I just crawl into my shell and feel sorry for myself. Maybe you've done that, too. I was sick inside about what had happened to Him and ashamed of myself that I hadn't done a thing to stop it. And what about God? Where was He when all that was happening?

On the first day of the week some crazy rumors began to circulate that the tomb was empty and some-one had taken away Jesus' body. The other disciples were planning to meet that night but I didn't want to be there. I just walked and walked, hardly knowing where I was going, hardly caring. What was the use of getting together again?

The next day, when I met Peter and John, they were all excited. They claimed that they had seen the Lord! It seemed a cruel kind of joke to me. As far as I was concerned they had a pretty sick sense of humor. But they kept insisting it was true. I wouldn't believe them,

I didn't dare. I'd been hurt so much by His dying that that I couldn't stand to get my hopes up again. But they wouldn't stop talking about it. "They must be seeing things," I thought. "They've gone out of their minds with grief." I felt myself getting angry. I wanted to lash out at them. "All right, you say He's alive; but I'm not going to believe it until I see the nailprints in His hands — until I touch them and put my hand in His side. Until I can do that, I'll never believe!"

That ended the conversation. I could tell I had hurt them, but I was in such a state that I didn't really care. It was too much to believe these wild dreams. I was irritated at the others, miserable myself, stubborn, and sick-hearted. But I stayed with the group, mainly because I didn't have anywhere else to go.

Then one night, about ten days after Jesus had died, the eleven of us were together again. I didn't feel close to the rest, so I was sitting off by myself, wondering what in the world I was going to do next. Suddenly, without any noise or warning, He was there in the room. We heard that familiar greeting again: "Shalom; peace be with you." No one else could say it like He did. Before I knew it, He was looking straight at me. Those eyes again. Slowly He walked over to me and spoke. "Put your finger here and see My hands and put out your hand and place it in My side. Do not be faithless but believing." That went through me like a sword. Can you imagine what it was like to hear my angry, stubborn, foolish words coming back at me from Him? I was embarrassed, ashamed — terribly ashamed. I wanted just to disappear or slip through the floor. I could hardly look at Him. But still I was overwhelmed that He knew all about me and my stubborn unbelief, and yet He came just for me. Even though I felt like a fool, joy just swept over me in a big wave when it dawned on me that He was alive. At that moment everything fell into place: the claims He had made for Himself, the beautiful life that He lived, His strange death, and now His coming back. I could see what it all meant. I knew then who He was. I fell on my face at His feet and the words came pouring out: "My Lord and my God!"

A lot has happened since then. After those early days in Jerusalem, the Spirit of God led me to bring the good news to Persia and finally here to India. I haven't seen Him now with my eyes for almost forty years, but I've learned now to trust when I can't see.

Maybe some of you sometimes feel as I felt. You have doubts that He really did rise from the dead. Other people say so, but you think they're just gullible. It's not easy for you to believe. You insist on having your own kind of proof. Well, I want you to know that He doesn't reject you because of that. And if you stay with His people and keep your mind open, one of these days you're going to meet Him. He'll make Himself real to you. And then He'll be saying again, "Do not be faithless but believing. Blessed are those who have not seen and yet believe." That's the great believing, isn't it? I hope that will happen for you and that you'll say as I said on that unforgettable day, "My Lord and my God!" I was quite a skeptic but the living Christ made a believer out of me. He can do that for you. Take it from me — the man they call "Doubting Thomas." And peace be with you.

QUESTIONS FOR DISCUSSION

1. In the light of the biblical record, how would you describe Thomas' character?

2. From his experience, what would you say is one of the *worst* things to do when we are depressed?

3. What does it say about us when we demand our own special brand of evidence?

4. From this whole record (including Jesus' final word, v. 29), what conclusions do you come to about the relationship between "seeing" and "believing"?

29. The Crucial Question

When they had finished breakfast, Jesus said to Simon Peter, "Simon, son of John, do you love me more than these?" He said to him, "Yes, Lord; you know that I love you." He said to him, "Feed my lambs." A second time he said to him, "Simon, son of John, do you love me?" He said to him, "Yes, Lord; you know that I love you." He said to him, "Tend my sheep." He said to him the third time, "Simon, son of John, do you love me?" Peter was grieved because he said to him the third time, "Do you love me?" And he said to him, "Lord, you know everything; you know that I love you." Jesus said to him, "Feed my sheep."

(John 21:15-17)

How WOULD YOU feel if you had failed your best friend at a time when he needed you most? Suppose that when the pressure was on, you had sworn up and down that you never even knew him. And suppose this all happened right after you had pledged your loyalty to him and promised that you'd never let him down. You'd said that you would stick with him even if everyone else turned away. And now see what you've done! How do you feel about that?

On the way out of court on the day of his trial, he looked at you, and that look was more than you could take. You had to get alone — fast — and the bitter tears came pouring out. You've seen him since and you know he's forgiven you, but you still have a hard time living with yourself. How do you begin life again after you've done something like that?

Simon Peter must have battled with those feelings. Easter, with its overwhelming joy, had come and gone. Peter, along with the rest, had seen the Lord; but now nothing had happened for several days and time was heavy on his hands. He decided to go fishing and took several of the other disciples along. It seemed like old times again — leaning into those oars, spotting the well-known landmarks, delighting even in the smell of a familiar boat. But this proved to be a long night on the big lake. They fished in all the best spots but came up with nothing. Peter had a lot of time to think.

What memories must have come flooding back! There was the day when he had first met Jesus by that same shore. He remembered another time when fishing was poor, and how Jesus had told him to go out deeper for a catch. Minutes later they had been swamped with fish! What a sense of awe had come over him then! Soon he had left the fishing boat behind to follow Jesus wherever He went. How could he ever forget those exciting tours in Galilee, especially that day when he first confessed his own faith in Jesus as God's Messiah? How high his hopes were then! How sure he was about everything!

But then came those words about Jesus' suffering. The storm clouds of opposition seemed to gather as they moved toward Jerusalem. He remembered with a twinge of pain how Jesus had washed his feet in that upper room. He, Peter, had wanted to be washed completely — anything that would make him altogether Christ's man. But soon after, he heard a word that shook him to the depths. He was told plainly that he was about to deny his Master. Peter winced as he recalled how he had protested. But the nightmare of those last hours — that was what, more than anything else, kept coming back. What could ever erase that from his memory? Years at the old fishing trade would never do it. Something had spoiled him now for that. But what good was he for anything else? Jesus was risen, yes. There was work to be done for Him. But how could Peter be trusted with it after what happened in the high priest's courtyard? As the night wore on and the fish stayed away, Simon Peter must have felt as empty as his nets. That was the story of his life — bright hopes, big plans, but nothing to show for it all.

When dawn was just beginning to frame the hills with pink and gold, the fishermen heard a voice from the beach: "Did you catch anything?" "No," they said, as only fishermen can say it. Who was this man, up so early, shouting across the water? Now He had a word of advice: "Cast the net on the right side of the boat and you'll find some." Someone groaned, "What a joke! All night we haven't been near a fish and now we're supposed to catch some right on the other side of the boat!" "Well, maybe He's seen something," said another; "what have we got to lose?" So they hauled up the nets one more time and swished them over the other side. Immediately they felt the old strain on the cords as the boat dipped low into the water. They couldn't even bring the nets back up!

John was the first to understand what was happening. He looked at Peter and said, "It's the Lord." That was all Simon Peter needed to hear. He snatched a cloak from the bottom of the boat and leaped into the water, thrashing for the shore. The rest of the disciples finally succeeded in dragging their monstrous catch up onto the sand. Sure enough, the figure on the beach was Jesus! And He had a fire going, with breakfast on the way. Talk about old times! The disciples felt awkward, though. They didn't know what to say. What was He doing here? What did this all mean? As they ate together, no one spoke. But how good everything tasted — especially after they hadn't expected much for breakfast!

As the meal was ending, the Lord turned toward Peter and spoke softly, "Simon, son of John, do you love me more than these?" You could almost feel the silence now. Peter looked up when he heard his name, then down at his big hands and up again. There was hurt in his eyes as he answered, "Yes, Lord; you know that I love you." Jesus seemed to be weighing those words. Then came the crisp command, "Feed my lambs." Each of the other disciples was feeling edgy. Was He going around the circle? Would each have to answer to Him? What will He say to me?

But He was still looking at Peter. Soon He was asking him again, this time more briefly, "Simon, son of John, do you love me?" Peter was even more uncomfortable now. His answer was slower in coming but when he finally got it out it was just the same: "Yes, Lord; you know that I love you." Then they heard the commission repeated: "Tend my sheep." But that didn't end it. Moments later Christ spoke again — almost as though He had never asked the question before, "Simon, son of John, do you love me?" By this time Peter was all choked up. Was his word good for nothing now? Could he never be trusted again? "Lord, you know everything; you know that I love you." Now the others could sense that the strange scene was ending. Jesus said it one more time, in a voice that seemed joyous and friendly, "Feed my sheep."

That was a pretty hard thing to put Peter through, wasn't it? What a wealth of pathos in that interchange! Think of those words: "Do you love me more than these?" That had been Peter's claim — others might forsake the Lord, but not he. "I will lay down my life for you," he had promised. What about it, Peter? Is yours really deeper and stronger than the love of these others? Peter no longer makes that kind of claim. He speaks now only for himself.

There was a poignancy, too, in the threefold question — piercing reminder of three crass denials. And imagine the embarrassment of being questioned like that in front of all the others!

But if all that was tough, it was a tough kind of love. To be faced and probed by those we've injured may be a hard thing, but it is a healing one, too. Resentment may write off a faithless friend, may shun him, ignore him, leave him to stew in what he's done, but love can't let him go. Love has to find him and win him back. Here is Jesus giving Peter another chance to say, "Lord, I do love You." He wants him to say it out. The denial was public; let the new confession be out in the open, too.

Notice how Peter answers. How would you have handled that if you were in his place? Could he say, "Lord, look how much I've done for You"? Hardly. No past favors look very convincing after you've sworn that you don't even know someone. And he couldn't appeal to his friends for an endorsement, either. They knew all too well what he had done. No, Peter went to the right place with his appeal — straight to the Lord's own heart. "You know, Lord: You know everything; You know that I love You." It's almost as though he's saying, "I know it doesn't seem like it, Lord. I know my life sometimes seems to deny it. I can't understand the way I act sometimes. But I know this, Lord, and You know it too, that in spite of everything I really meant what I said."

It's good to have that final court of appeal, isn't it? When failure and forgetfulness seem to make a mockery of our devotion, when cowardice and compromise make us out as hypocrites rather than disciples, it's good to know that He sees some spark of love still alive down beneath it all. And how gracious He is to let us tell Him about it!

The same mercy shines in His commission: "Feed my lambs . . . tend my sheep." You could read it as a kind of ultimatum, a last-chance mandate: "Do this or else!" But Peter didn't see it that way. For him the command was all grace. It was good news, sweet music.

Christ was giving him his apostleship back again. There, in front of the others, Peter was being reinstated. Now he had purpose again, something to live for. And best of all, it meant that he was trusted, trusted in spite of everything. Here was a new opportunity, another chance to serve the One he really loved.

Now where does all of this find you, especially that question with your own name in it, "Simon, son of John, do you love me?" It's a simple question, but oh, what a big one! Nothing says more about any of us than how we respond to the greatest love that ever touches our lives. Our answer to the love that came in a manger and died on a cross is the truest measure of what we are.

You may say, "But I don't need that question. I never denied Christ like Peter did." Are you sure of that? Is there nothing about your life that seems to disown Him? Or, to look at it another way, what evidence is there on the positive side? What demonstrates the genuineness of your love? You say you're a church member, a leader perhaps, knowledgeable about Scripture, active in many good causes? Fine, but none of that makes the question unnecessary. Peter was all of that, and more. And how many marriages are there in which people still go through the motions long after real caring has died? No, if we profess to follow Christ at all, the question is for us, too. Do we love Him — not with the love of sentiment alone, but with a desire to please Him in everything? And this is not a question we can answer once and for all. One profession of love is not enough to last a lifetime in any relationship. The question keeps coming back. Christ comes all the way from His glory to ask it of one man, and he's asking it still.

It's the crucial question — crucial in the real sense — a question with a cross in the middle of it. You and I didn't deny Him on the night before He died, but the evils that made His cross necessary are very much ours. The love that stood in our place there and carried our load is the power behind His question, "Do you love me?" And the answer we give makes a crucial difference — the difference between authentic Christianity and a pale counterfeit.

If you've been gripped by His love, if you can say in spite of all your treachery and hollowness, "Lord, You know I love You," then He has a work for you to do — caring for the sheep in His fold and seeking the ones who've wandered away. No matter how much you've failed, He's not through with you. He sends you afresh to express His shepherd-love toward others.

But the question is very personal, isn't it? We have to answer it directly to Him. One Christian who must have known how Peter felt responded in the words of a beautiful hymn. Maybe it says what you want to say: "Lord, it is my chief complaint that my love is weak and faint; Yet I love Thee and adore — Oh, for grace to love Thee more!"

QUESTIONS FOR DISCUSSION

1. What does this passage teach us about the differing gifts and temperaments of Peter and John?

2. Was it unkind of Jesus to question Peter about his devotion when the other disciples were present? Discuss.

3. What was the special appropriateness of Peter's reply?

4. Why does the question have continuing relevance and importance for us?

30. Concentrate On This

"Truly, truly, I say to you, when you were young, you girded yourself and walked where you would; but when you are old, you will stretch out your hands, and another will gird you and carry you where you do not wish to go." (This he said to show by what death he was to glorify God.) And after this he said to him, "Follow me." Peter turned and saw following them the disciple whom Jesus loved, who had lain close to his breast at the supper and had said, "Lord, who is it that is going to betray you?" When Peter saw him, he said to Jesus, "Lord, what about this man?" Jesus said to him, "If it is my will that he remain until I come, what is that to you? Follow me!"

(John 21:18-22)

Do you ever feel scattered, pulled apart by the multitude of demands made on you? So many different voices seem to be calling, urging you this way and that. At times you feel like that proverbial rider who jumped on his horse and rode off in all directions at once! Do you ever wish that life could be simplified; that the endless profusion of duties could somehow be gathered into one? You'd like someone to do for your life's responsibilities what the finance companies do with your bills — pay all of them off so you just have one major obligation remaining. Sounds attractive, doesn't it? Wouldn't it be great if we had just one thing to concentrate on in life so that everything else would settle into its proper place!

I get the feeling that many people are looking for that: an authoritative word that makes sense out of all our other duties — something really worth doing, some call supremely worth heeding, some overarching allegiance that will pull everything together. But is there anything like that? Is there such a call? And is there anyone big enough to sound it? Christians answer yes on all three counts. They have found that unifying factor in the simple call of Jesus Christ: "Follow me." This is the one thing they have to do.

What did Jesus mean when He called people to follow Him? The terminology was familiar enough. Anyone knew what following was. It meant "going behind" someone. And in the ancient world to follow the gods meant to imitate them — to do what they did. But Jesus never urged His disciples to copy everything He did. They did not, for example, remain bachelors, nor did they confine their ministry to Palestine, nor did they die for the sins of the world and rise again three days later! With Jesus the basic idea was definitely not imitation.

The idea of following a rabbi, or teacher, was also a familiar one in Israel. Every rabbi had his pupils whom he led in religious discussions or study classes in the Torah. Young men would follow a rabbi for a certain period of time, hoping eventually to become better rabbis than their teacher. But that idea would have been inconceivable to those who followed Jesus. They saw Him as unique. No rabbi had ever issued a call so radical and personal.

Following Jesus was seen from the first as an all-absorbing commitment. It was the kind of total allegiance to which that fiery prophet Elijah once summoned the people on Mount Carmel. "How long will you go limping with two different opinions?" he cried.

"If the LORD is God follow him; but if Baal, then follow him" (1 Kings 18:21). Here "following" plainly means supreme devotion, complete self-dedication.

And it was that way with Christ's call. When He summoned men, they left their nets and followed Him. They left their boats — and even their relatives — to walk behind Him. The old attachments were no longer binding in the same way. When would-be disciples wanted to care for other responsibilities before they followed Jesus, He gave them no leeway. The call to follow had produced a new situation. The first step was a break with the past. Nothing else claimed priority now.

But this "burning of the boats," as it were, had no meaning in itself. It was simply the reverse side of a new loyalty, a new relationship to Jesus Himself. "Following" was a personal attachment to Him which transcended all former ties. To follow Him was to be identified with Him. It involved knowing, but a knowledge not primarily of ideas but of a person. It meant obedience, but this was rendered not to a code of rules but to a living Lord. And the faith it expressed was first of all a personal trust in Jesus. Everything else in life was to be grounded on that — belonging to Him.

This personal dimension becomes clear when the risen Christ, about to ascend to His Father, still calls one of His disciples to follow. Peter will no longer be walking behind Him in the fields of Galilee, or on Judean roads, but the call is still the same. The relationship continues, in an even deeper way. For us, too, following Christ is the one thing needful in *all* the seasons of life. Listen to this word to Peter: "Truly, truly I say to you, when you were young, you girded yourself and walked where you would; but when you are old, you will stretch out your hands, and another will gird you and carry you where you do not wish to go." In youth we are heady with an awareness of our powers and possibilities. We feel that nothing is beyond our reach. We are ready for anything. In rugged Peter, often acting before he thinks, pulling his sword to fight for Christ, leaping out of a fishing boat to meet Him, we have a vivid picture of youth — full of energy, hurling itself into new adventures. What a time that is for following Christ!

But life has other seasons, too. Peter learns that one day, being old, he will find his life determined by forces beyond his control. Those who are getting on in years know what that is all about. We begin to reevaluate our gifts and potential. We lay aside some extravagant dreams, and settle for more modest aims. Forced to reckon with our limitations, we feel the future narrowing around us. We are not nearly so independent as once we thought we were. But in those times, too, following Christ makes life meaningful. We walk behind Him as we dare and do, but also as we simply endure. "They also serve who only stand and wait."

I was looking the other day at several pictures gathered for a magazine article. They represent, by an assortment of chairs, the stages of life through which all of us pass. We see first a highchair, then a school desk with books on it, then a swivel seat in an office. Next comes an easy chair with newspaper and slippers, then a rocker, and finally a wheelchair. So our lives go. But it doesn't really matter from which chair we first rise to answer His call. Following Him, once begun, can be the business of a whole lifetime.

For Peter the idea of streaching out his hands and being carried where he didn't want to go had a meaning deeper than old age. Here Jesus was speaking in veiled language about the apostle's death, the death by which "he was to glorify God." Peter had already learned that following Christ meant *service:* feeding sheep and tending lambs, caring for those who are precious to Christ. Now he is reminded that *suffering* lies ahead. That's what we find hard to accept about following Christ. If we can be accomplishing something, influencing others, actively obeying, that seems like real discipleship. But when we are sick, hemmed in by circumstances, weakened by age, or when sore trials lay us low, it's hard to realize that we can be following Christ then. But right here is the great comfort of this attachment to Him. It doesn't depend on performance or production, at least in the outward sense. When following Christ is the aim of life, even patient suffering is real discipleship and death itself can give praise to God. Whatever you go through, you go through it with Him and for Him.

But there is still another sense in which to concentrate on following Christ enriches and purifies our lives. It keeps us from the distraction of looking around at others. Peter had just heard his Lord's commission. He had been told of the path of service and suffering that lay ahead for him and had been called afresh to follow. But soon he looked behind him and saw John following. Peter wondered about the Lord's plan for his fellow disciple. "Lord, what about this man?" he asked. Jesus' answer brought him up short: "If it is my will that he remain until I come, what is that to you? Follow me."

How much Christ communicates in those brief words! The phrase "If I will that he remain" points to the Lord's final control over the lives of His people. They remain active in this world as His followers so long as He wills it. Their days, their times, their ministries are in His hands. His grand purpose is being worked out in the life of each servant. And here is the main point: how He deals with another brother or sister is *His* business and not ours.

This habit of looking around at other disciples is one of the most distracting things a Christian can do. Perhaps we have known suffering and heartbreak in our family circle, while the homes of other believers seem almost untouched by sorrow. We wonder why. Or someone else with similar background and training seems to be far more successful in his work than we are. Everything he touches turns to gold, but we have a continual struggle. We're tempted to ask, "What about this man?" Friends of ours perhaps can witness with great joy and naturalness; some are amazingly fruitful in their evangelistic labors, while we seem to have such meager influence where we live and work. We begin to look at those others with a jaundiced eye, to feel uneasy in their presence, to wonder why our lot is so much more difficult or limited. But when we feel that way, as Peter did, we need to hear again the Lord's searching word: "What is that to you? Follow me."

Whenever we begin to question what is happening in other lives we have badly lost the way. Our eyes aren't on Christ any more. Soon we fall even farther behind Him, and life loses its joy and purpose. So the call of Jesus, "Follow me," though it sounds like a rebuke, is really a benediction. It frees and redirects us, calling to mind what we're in the world for, and pointing to the One whose opinion matters. We stop then trying to "play God" or serve as an amateur providence. We get our eyes once again fixed on the goal.

But it's hard to stay with that, isn't it? It's hard to be like Caleb, that Old Testament worthy, of whom it was said so often that he "wholly followed the Lord." Our lives often seem to be characterized more by looking around than by pressing on, more by wandering than by following. Certainly that was true of those first disciples. After three years of learning to follow Jesus, they failed when the big test came. They all forsook Him and ran away.

Was His training program a failure? Did His call, after all, end in nothing? No, but it took His cross and resurrection to make real following possible. It was after that victory that He could come to someone like Peter — or like you and me — and say, "All right now, follow Me." Even though we are weak the One who summons us is strong. "Follow me and I will make you fishers of men," He promises. The one who calls us also re-creates our lives. He makes possible our ministry as His servants. He delivers us from every distraction, so that in spite of ourselves we stay with Him.

That's why the call of Jesus Christ is all-sufficient for our lives. It points to a high road, a path of duty and discipleship to walk in. But it promises even more: His own companionship, grace for the wanderer, strength for the way. Are you looking for something to pull a scattered life together? Jesus Christ has a way. In fact, He *is* the way.

Whatever your stage in life, whatever your strength or struggle, whether you feel like a leader or an also-ran, His call can get you on the right track. So stop trying to plot someone else's course. The Lord is asking, loud and clear, "What is that to you? Follow me!"

QUESTIONS FOR DISCUSSION

1. What kind of commitment is ultimately involved in "following" Jesus?

2. Hadn't Peter been following Him for years? What is the significance of the renewed command?

3. What other forms of "following" are there besides active service and witness?

4. What are the dangers involved in comparing ourselves with other Christians and questioning God's dealings with them?